Jerome S. Stumphauzer

Behavio

Modification

Principles

Designed and
Illustrated
by Mike Frazier

Jerome S. Stumphauzer

Behavior Modification Principles

An Introduction and Training Manual

Behaviordelia, Inc.
Kalamazoo, Michigan

International Standard Book Number:
0-914-47422-7

Library of Congress Cataloging in Publication Data:
1. Behavior modification. I. Title.
BF637.B4S83 153.8'5 76-49229

PO Box 1044
Kalamazoo, Michigan 49005

1 2 3 4 5 6 7 8 9
5 4 3 2 1 0 9 8 7

Contents

Foreword

Virtually every high school graduate prides himself or herself on the possession of an instinctive ability to know and understand something about people, and what makes them tick. In the heyday of the Freudian era, it was also accepted that most people were amateurs in this process and that, to appreciate the complex depths of man's functioning, it was necessary to have a profound understanding of unconscious forces which only the expert, the psychodynamically trained specialist, could possibly know about. Even the most sophisticated armchair Freudian knew his place and left the mystique in all its glory to the professional psychotherapist or psychoanalyst.

The relatively recent advent of behavior therapy – a term which we use here more or less synonymously with behavior modification – produced radical changes in this mode of thinking. No longer did the principles of human interaction lie primarily in the domain of the specialist in depth psychology. In those early, halcyon days of behavior therapy, less than a decade and a half ago, the shift was to the other extreme. All became simple, cut-and dried, with little room for ifs, buts and equivocation. It is the ironic fate of all rebels to end up founding orthodoxies of their own and, in rebelling against the orthodoxy of traditional psychodynamic thinking, these early behavior therapists were no exception.

In the 30's J.B. Watson grandiosely attempted to change the face of American psychology and to solve mankind's besetting social and economic ills by banishing all forms of introspection and any evidence of cognitive processes to an arbitrarily declared state of nonexistence. In the late 50's and early 60's certain equally naive and brash behavior therapists followed a similar path. In both eras, reactions from the public at large and their more sophisticated colleagues in the mental health professions were resolutely adverse.

The similarities between this aspect of the behavior therapy climate of the late 50's and early 60's and the era of J.B. Watson are striking. Both were characterized by oversimplification, pontification, intolerance, mechanistic terminology, fervent evangelism and precariously founded generalizations. Inner forces, on the one hand, and extra-psychological determinants on the other, were denied or regarded as irrelevant. There was an optimistic belief – quite extraordinary when viewed with the convenient hindsight of the 70's – that all that was needed to bring about the brave new world typified by such distinguished writers as Aldous Huxley, H.G. Wells and even B.F. Skinner himself, was a practical knowledge of the simple principles of classical and operant conditioning. Family units, social organizations, societal and ethical issues, and the contributions of disciplines or data derived from other schools of thought were regarded as of little or no concern. Life was deceptively simple and straightforward, with no reason or room for doubt, complication, second thoughts or anything beyond the straightening confines of the simple S-R paradigm.

The situation today is different, and yet not so different. Behavior therapy is alive and well and living in vigorous strength everywhere; and yet oversimplification and ill-considered enthusiasm still abound. It tends to attract those who seek seemingly easy routes to fame and fortune without an understanding of what behavior therapy is all about. For such individuals, behavior therapy is little more than the application of a few readily acquired techniques which can be applied by virtually anyone regardless of training or orientation. Such individuals are "trained" – a euphemism if ever there were one – in short-term workshops which qualify them as specialists in assertion training, behavior therapy in management, anxiety reduction, biofeedback techniques and anything else the behavioral entrepreneurs can dream up. The implication is that by the simple utilization of such procedures almost all the world's ills can be corrected, ranging from conditioned alpha for the elimination of acne and mental stress to the resolution of interracial tensions or the problems of pollution and litter control by token economies.

No wonder then that the lay public and the nonbehavioral professional react with distaste and rejection. Those who stress technology – and often pseudotechnology at that – rather than understanding, and mechanistic process rather than human freedom and dignity, are sometimes the more vociferous among our ranks even though they do not represent the majority. These individuals, neither well-trained behavioral scientists nor sensitive clinicians, are prone to rush into print, workshops or public lectures with little or no thought or even care for the consequences.

Fortunately, all is not as dismal as this portrayal might suggest. On the positive side, there are the activities of the cautious and responsible majority, well trained as both behavioral scientists and clinicians. Behavior therapy is far more than a grab bag of gimmicks and the practice of a few behavioral procedures. A vendor of techniques does not a behavior therapist make. Behavior therapy is a methodological prescription rather than a school of thought. The hallmark of this methodology is an objective and systematic analysis – something psychoanalysts seem to overlook – followed by controlled, monitored intervention amid a process of continual evaluation and accountability.

This year is the 300th anniversary of one of the more important aphorisms in the history of science and culture. On February 18, 1676, Sir Isaac Newton stated, "If I have seen further, it is by standing on the shoulders of giants." This applies not only to the natural sciences but to the growth of knowledge in every area of learning. Perhaps the overriding difference in the case of behavior therapy is that the giant is rarely – if ever – a product of any single individual or any one breakthrough. The giant is that reservoir of painstakingly accumulated, data-oriented units of information put together by an array of behavioral scientists who pave the way for each subsequent investigator.

Foremost among such up-and-coming behavioral scientists is Dr. Jerry Stumphauzer, a dedicated researcher and clinical investigator who knows well that breakthroughs, deceptively seductive program packages and technique innovations operating primarily at the notional level are the very antithesis of what contemporary behavior therapy is all about. The competent behavior therapist of the 70's is cautious, unassuming, concerned with analysis of data rather than psyches and open to alternative hypotheses and the recognition of the limitations of what he or she is trying to accomplish.

This unpretentious new book by Dr. Stumphauzer exemplifies the best in this tradition. His goals are modest and clearly delineated: to present behavior therapy within the perspective of the behavioral scientist; to inculcate the reader with a healthy respect both for its successes and its limitations; to offer a clear statement of the principles of behavior therapy and their applications. Most importantly, the structure of the book itself is predicated upon the principles of behavior modification. Modeling, feedback and learning by doing are stressed; the reader is expected to become an active participant by experiencing what it is like to design and implement some behavioral program of his or her choice. Formal instruction, further reading and the opportunity for discussion and interaction with an experienced behavior therapist would enhance the value of this training experience yet further.

This is not to say that this book could only be used in the above fashion. It is so planned that it could stand alone as an introduction to behavior therapy. It could provide an overview of what forward-looking behavior therapists do and thus offer a greater appreciation and understanding of these activities. It might also serve as a starting-off point for a decision to enroll in some appropriate doctoral training program.

This is one of the few basic texts that I know of which offers these opportunities in a form which is concise, clear and enjoyable to read. But then, I would not have expected anything less from such an individual as Dr. Jerome Stumphauzer – a good behavioral scientist, a competent clinician and an empathetic human being. Ultimately, the extent to which this book achieves its goals will depend on how much you, the reader, put into it.

Cyril M. Franks, PhD
Professor
Graduate School of Applied and Professional Psychology
Rutgers University
November, 1976

Preface

PURPOSE

In first learning and then teaching behavior modification and therapy over the last several years, I have been struck by the repeated mention of behavior modification "principles," but never by seeing a list or a brief, clear presentation of such principles. I thought such a list would be especially helpful to the new student of behavior modification, so in 1971 I began compiling one. While a list of principles has been useful as a key to learning behavior modification and therapy, it alone was not enough. In spite of the fact that there are several introductions to behavior modification, I believed that these principles were not available to students and instructors in a concise text, and I set this as my goal. In the present volume I have: 1) given the principles perspective by including an introduction to history and issues; 2) added a program to teach each principle; 3) provided modeling of the application of each principle with both children and adults; and, 4) given the reader or student an opportunity to practice using each principle.

The intent has been to provide a book that is very concise and brief (the time required to work through the book currently varies from two to six hours). It is intended to stand on its own as an introduction or training manual, to be used in class, discussion or practicum, and possibly to be used in conjunction with another text, other readings, or practice and supervision.

AUDIENCE

This book is intended for a wide variety of readers – college students, trainees in workshops, teachers, counselors and therapists seeking a basic introduction or reference manual of behavior modification principles.

TO THE STUDENT

In first learning about behavior modification, you will find this book a useful guide for "nailing down" the most important principles of the field. While the "history" and "issues" sections are important for gaining perspective, you will find that the principles themselves are the key to first understanding and then changing behavior. Reading this book or learning these basic principles will not make you a behavior therapist; but it can provide a solid base for learning behavior therapy, especially in conjunction with other readings, practice and supervision.

TO THE TRAINEE

Your time for studying and learning new approaches is probably quite limited, and this probably includes the time you have available to learn about behavior modification. You will find that this book requires very little of your time, yet it actively involves you in learning practical principles for changing behavior. An attempt was made to make these principles "real" for you. You will find many of them immediately useful and a foundation for further training in behavior modification. This book was developed, in part, by responding to the needs and suggestions of trainees who learned these principles from an earlier draft of the book.

TO THE TEACHER, COUNSELOR OR THERAPIST

If you are already a teacher, counselor or therapist, you will find this book a useful study guide, reference and "idea" book for first learning the basic principles of behavior modification and then applying them in your daily work. Many of the modeled examples are from classrooms and clinical cases. This is not intended to be a "cookbook," however, and additional study and supervision will be needed.

TO THE INSTRUCTOR OR TRAINER

You will find this book a uniquely useful means of teaching basic behavior modification principles in a short time. You may wish to use it in conjunction with another text or a series of readings, observation, discussion and supervised practicum. The modeled examples of each principle were chosen, in part, because of their easy accessibility in most college or psychology libraries. You may wish to assign some of the full articles as readings.

While there are now a great many introductions to behavior modification, you will find this an unusually economical way to teach these basics. You may want to change the order of presentation or to utilize only those principles that fit your particular course or training program. The book may serve as a text or supplementary text in any course dealing with behavior modification (in psychology, psychiatry, education, social work, etc.).

The book has been used successfully as a basic training manual for paraprofessional community workers [Teicher, Sinay, & Stumphauzer, 1976 (see Introduction)], and probation officers [Burkhart, Behles, & Stumphauzer, 1976 (see Introduction)], with basically a "chapter a week" training format. Instructors and those doing training will find the *Practice Pages* serve well as homework, which you may wish to go over in detail, or as good springboards for small discussion groups.

ACKNOWLEDGEMENTS

This book has developed gradually with input from a great many people. Of course the principles themselves are not conceptually my creation. I attempted to formulate them in as concise a manner as possible while reflecting what I saw as consensus in current behavioral literature. There will undoubtedly be disagreement on the choice of principles and their wording, and I would appreciate suggestions for further clarifying them.

The researchers who have applied these principles successfully deserve major credit for teaching us by modeling their work. However, the briefness of the summaries in no way reflects the depth of their studies. I have chosen only the basic points from the research which demonstrate the particular principle you'll be learning. Readers serious about imitating these studies should seek out the original complete publications.

A few individuals must be mentioned for their important stimulation and feedback on earlier drafts of this book. Cyril M. Franks has generously given his encouragement and detailed suggestions for developing the book. A number of colleagues and students have reacted constructively to their experience with the book and added important suggestions for improvement: Ruth Sinay, Barbara Bishop, David deVidal, Robert Polakow, Barry Burkhart, Kent Candelora, Victor Sanchez, Thomas Aiken and Esteban Veloz.

Finally, the staff at Behaviordelia should be acknowledged for their active encouragement during the final development of the manuscript: Gerald Deegan, Bonnie Wolf, and Barb Swart. Mike Frazier's inspired cartoons add greatly to the book. I hope that they will not only provide entertainment and reinforcement for page turning, but also will add a further level of modeling through humor.

Jerome S. Stumphauzer
Los Angeles
December, 1976

ABOUT THE AUTHOR

Dr. Jerome Stumphauzer is an Associate Clinical Professor of Psychology and Psychiatry at the University of Southern California School of Medicine, where he does behavior modification training and research on a wide variety of problems from delinquency, autism and drug abuse, to prevention and community change. A Florida State University graduate, Dr. Stumphauzer has edited *Behavior Therapy with Delinquents* and *Progress in Behavior Therapy with Delinquents* (in press). In addition, he has published a wide variety of papers on training and treatment, developed two measurement devices (*Daily Behavior Card* and *Daily Behavior Graph*) and prepared an audio cassette, *Six Techniques of Modifying Delinquent Behavior.*

Basic Concepts

Chapter 1

Introduction

In general, behavior modification or behavior therapy may be defined as *the systematic application of the psychological* **principles** *of learning in modifying human behavior* (Wolpe, 1973, 1976a; Stumphauzer, 1973; Rimm & Masters, 1974). Several names have been given to this field: behavior modification, behavior therapy, conditioning therapy, etc. The term "behavior therapy" seems to have been coined independently by Skinner and Lindsley (1954), Lazarus (1958), and Eysenck (1959). Americans seem to have preferred the title "behavior modification" in the 1950's and 1960's, especially in reference to Skinnerian based approaches (Krasner & Ullmann, 1965; Ullmann & Krasner, 1965). This book will accept the more recent practice of using the terms "behavior modification" and "behavior therapy" interchangeably.

Behavior modification has experienced a phenomenal growth in the past 10 years. This is true for at least three major reasons. First, behavior modification has proven to be effective and economical in a wide variety of settings – from school classrooms to mental hospitals and the community. Second, there has been a gradual disenchantment with traditional psychotherapies, community programs and educational systems. Third, and by design, behavior modification can demonstrate its cause/effect results clearly, and this is increasingly asked for by funding agencies with their demands for "accountability" and "cost effectiveness."

Behavior modification principles are now widely applied in schools, hospitals, prisons, clinics and community programs. The field has grown so much that a review paper seems impossible, although Krasner's (1971) is an exception. For the more advanced student, two outstanding, thorough texts are Bandura's *Principles of Behavior Modification* (1969), and Kanfer and Phillips's *Learning Foundations of Behavior Therapy* (1970). Wolpe's clinical manuals (1973, 1976c), and Franks and Wilson's (1973-1976) *Annual Review of Behavior Therapy* series are also recommended. Numerous other good general and topic limited texts are available as well. An introduction is even available in "comic book" format (Malott & Hartlep, 1972).

A number of principles and techniques are taught and are in wide use. Although many books, manuals, and case studies have been published over the last several years, nowhere are the basic principles spelled out specifically (as such) in a clear, very brief, programmed introduction for the new student or practitioner of behavior therapy. This is the goal of this book.

Before turning to step-by-step instructions on how to use this book in learning the principles of behavior modification, two topics should be discussed. First, to put these principles in perspective, an historical review of the behavior modification movement is necessary. Second, a discussion of critical ethical and legal issues is important as a way of orienting you to some of the controversies facing behavior modification today.

HISTORY OF BEHAVIOR MODIFICATION

There are many accounts in ancient writings of what we would now call behavior modification, from Pliny the Elder discussing how to stop alcoholism by creating an aversion to drinking, to Socrates explaining that men do pleasurable things and avoid painful experiences. But this is behavior modification by hindsight: the labeling of activities in history with modern principles of learning which seem to have been inadvertently used. It was much later that *treatment* was actually *based on the science of learning.*

One beginning of behavior therapy may be traced to the experiments and writings of the Russian physiologist, Ivan Pavlov. Franks (1969) gives a full account of the importance of this work. Pavlov's (1927, 1928) classic studies of the conditioned reflex and the variables that control such conditioning were the groundwork for his later speculations on the part conditioning played in abnormal human behavior (1932, 1941), and much later for clinical application by others of his findings.

In America, Thorndike (1913) pioneered studies in problem solving and learning. His *law of effect* – behavior is learned because of its effect – remains a milestone. However, it was the work and personality of John B. Watson that finally gained wide attention. His book, *Behaviorism* (1924), with its radical position (at that time) on the human condition, established a direction that American psychologists still follow to a large degree. In addition, Watson and his colleagues made critical contributions to behavior therapy in their early studies. Watson and Rayner (1920) dramatically demonstrated learning of fear in a young child. Mary Cover Jones (1924), a student and colleague of Watson, is credited with the first true application of behavior therapy. Building on the work of Watson, she used his understanding of how fear was learned, in treating Peter, a young boy suffering from a fear of animals. In another early application of behavior therapy, Mowrer and Mowrer (1938) developed a technique for treating enuresis (placing an electrical circuit in a pad under the child that starts a bell once the bed is wetted) that is still widely used today.

For the next 20 to 30 years there was what appears to be a curious hiatus in the development of behavior modification. Franks (1969) reasonably explains this fallow period with the following reasoning. First, psychoanalysis was continuing to grow and become the center of attention for the therapeutic community which was largely dominated by psychiatry. Secondly, there was no one to practice behavior therapy. Watson, Jones and Mowrer were mainly academic psychologists; there were no clinical psychologists as we know them today. There was no one who both understood the psychological process of learning and tried to apply this knowledge directly in clinical practice. However, something critical to behavior therapy was going on during this period. Academic psychologists were developing what came to be called *learning theories*. Careful, critical experiments and resulting theories were developing which provided a scientific understanding of behavior based upon controlled research, and formed the principles of learning for later researchers to amplify, and for behavior therapists to apply clinically.

From the end of World War II to the middle 1950's there was a profound change in the field of psychiatry, and especially in clinical psychology. Many new training sites and jobs opened for psychologists (e.g., Veterans Administration Hospitals). Even though psychologists were in positions subordinate to those of psychiatrists, they began to critically question the foundations, assumptions and wide applicability of the psychiatric approach in general, and psychoanalytic practice in particular (Yates, 1970). The disease concept of mental illness, while perhaps congruent with medical training, did not seem to adequately account for either understanding problems in living or helping people improve (Szasz, 1961, has since been the outspoken, eloquent critic of the "myth of mental illness").

Psychologists with their background in research, began to investigate psychiatric diagnosing and to find negative data on reliability and validity. More important, they began to demonstrate that psychotherapy was no more effective than the complete absence of treatment, or even that it was detrimental (Eysenck, 1952)! Psychodynamic treatment, developed from the work of Freud, with its foundations in hypothetical, mental constructs (e.g., id, ego, superego), its speculative formulation from individual patients and its scientifically untestable hypotheses, came increasingly under criticism. In fact, behavior therapy has developed, in part, as a reaction against, and an alternative to psychodynamic treatment. Dollard and Miller (1950) attempted to translate psychoanalytic concepts into scientific learning terms, but their work only resulted in a further confusion of clinical practice still based upon unscientific theorizing. Salter's (1949) early book, *Conditioned Reflex Therapy,* did come closer to what was becoming behavior therapy, with its more direct utilization of Pavlov's conditioning principles in understanding and treating patients.

In the late 1950's three separate developments, in three parts of the world, were all leading toward modern behavior therapy. It is important to understand that behavior therapy did not rise from one source, and this helps to explain some of the issues which will be discussed later. In the United States, B.F. Skinner (1938, 1953) was having a profound effect on American psychology. His research on learning (operant conditioning), his method of clearly demonstrating cause/effect relationships in individual organisms (experimental analysis of behavior), and the wide-ranging work of his prolific students, all contributed to methods of understanding and changing behavior which were forming a base of established principles.

In an early novel, *Walden II* (1948), Skinner was suggesting that society's "good life" could be based upon utilizing the scientific understanding of behavior. In the late 1950's, psychologists were beginning to seriously try just that, first with hospitalized patients (Lindsley & Skinner, 1954; Ferster & DeMyer, 1961), and later in educational programs (Baer & Wolf, 1968). Ayllon and Azrin (1965, 1968) began a series of experiments in a state psychiatric hospital, developing a "token economy" where learning principles were applied directly in a programmed environment for hospitalized patients. Others in America began applying learning principles in many diverse clinical and educational settings; they called this new approach behavior modification.

In South Africa, Joseph Wolpe (1952) was experimentally demonstrating that neurotic kinds of behavior in animals were indeed learned behavior (work also pioneered by Masserman, 1943). Wolpe reasoned that neurotic anxiety and fear are also learned in humans, and therefore, learning principles should be utilized in treatment. In his hallmark book, *Psychotherapy by Reciprocal Inhibition* (1958), he developed his case further with supportive clinical cases and scientific data (see Chapter 16).

Independently, a group of clinical researchers in England, at the Institute of Psychiatry and at the Maudsley Hospital, headed by Hans J. Eysenck and Michael B. Shapiro, were also adding to the early development of behavior therapy. On the one hand they were doing research which was severely critical of traditional psychotherapy (Eysenck, 1952); and on the other hand, they were beginning to utilize learning in individual therapy cases in an experimental manner, i.e. demonstrating and verifying cause and effect relationships (Yates, 1970). The early work of this English group culminated in the development of the first journal devoted exclusively to this area (*Behaviour Research and Therapy,* 1963) with Eysenck as the Editor-in-Chief.

The 1960's witnessed a proliferation of behavior modification. There was an explosion of literature on the topic with articles and books increasing rapidly (Ernst, 1971). Early presentations took the form of single case studies in which basic principles were demonstrated with every conceivable kind of patient and behavior. Patterson (1971a) has called this period the "whoopie phase" in the development of behavior therapy, and critically called for its end since there was no longer any doubt that such principles "worked." The need, he insisted, was for more critical evaluations of widely applied principles or for systematic, long-term investigation aimed at cumulative progress. As early as 1969, Dr. Gordon Paul found that such an "experimental era" had already begun successfully.

In the 1960's, behavior therapy was demonstrated to be effective with a wide variety of populations and behaviors. One especially fruitful application has been in education (Baer & Wolf, 1968). Other areas are psychiatric hospital token economies (Ayllon & Azrin, 1968; Kazdin & Bootzin, 1972), psychiatric nursing (Schaefer & Martin,

1969), behavior therapy techniques (Franks, 1974; Ullmann & Krasner, 1965; Wolpe & Lazarus, 1966), and research in behavior therapy (Krasner & Ullmann, 1965; Franks, 1969).

In the 1960's Albert Bandura brought our attention to social learning, the importance of exposure to models, and learning through imitation (1962, 1969, 1975). Lazarus (1968) split from what was tradition at that time and took a position of "broad spectrum" or "multimodal" behavior therapy wherein *any* technique that results in behavior improvement can and should be used. Wolpe (1969) strongly objected to this "unscientific" brand of behavior therapy, and both remain adamant to this day (Lazarus, 1971; Wolpe, 1973, 1976b).

In 1968 the *Journal of Applied Behavior Analysis* made its appearance as the standard bearer of the Skinnerian approach to "applied" problems. The classic article by Baer, Wolf, and Risley (1968) defined the dimensions of American behavior modification following Skinner's experimental analysis of behavior. During this period the education of psychologists, and later, psychiatrists, was beginning to include and even, in some cases, to be dominated by the behavior modification or behavior therapy approach (see especially *Psychology Today,* 1972, November, for a description of the "who" and "where" of behavior modification in the 1960's and early 1970's).

Behavior modification more logically drew from psychological training with its dual emphasis on learning and research. It gave psychologists an identity and expertise quite apart from the previous role of "pseudopsychiatrist" and "tester" (Yates, 1970). Conflicts between the psychodynamic approach and the behavioral approach continued in this period. Psychodynamic theorists suggested that the naive approach of simply treating "symptoms" (behaviors) while ignoring inner "causes" would not result in lasting change, or, at least, would necessarily lead to "symptom substitution." The literature over these years does not support any notion of substitution of behaviors or of temporary results. This period also saw various unsuccessful attempts to marry psychoanalysis and behavior therapy, but the separation continues (Wolpe, 1976b).

The 1970's thus far have provided both success and critical new problems along with growth. Behavior modification has increased in scope and impact, but has also come face to face with ethical and legal issues which will be presented in more detail later. Two international organizations have developed for behavior therapists. They are the *Association for Advancement of Behavior Therapy* (with its journal, *Behavior Therapy*) and the *Behavior Therapy and Research Society*. A fourth journal has also made its appearance, the *Journal of Behavior Therapy and Experimental Psychiatry*; and a fifth journal, *Behavior Modification*, will start in 1977.

The American Psychiatric Association appointed a blue ribbon panel to study behavior therapy and its potential contribution to psychiatry. They concluded that principles of behavior therapy . . . "now unquestionably have much to offer informed clinicians in the service of modern clinical and social psychiatry" (Birk et al., 1973, p. 64). This more or less "official" acceptance by the American Psychiatric Association may begin to put an end to the psychology/psychiatry split over behavior therapy.

Behavior modification has taken on many "new directions" in the 1970's. Krasner (1971) suggests that in the future behavior therapy research will both "go further *inside* the organism by relating autonomic and neurological functioning to the behavior change process, and further *outward* to the multivariable of the social environment" (p. 518). To some extent this is already the case. Biofeedback, the control of visceral learning by conditioning procedures, is now receiving a great deal of attention (Miller, 1969, 1972). This "going inside" has also included modification of cognitive processes. The cognitive behavior modification of Meichenbaum is exemplary (1971, 1973, 1975). Also, the rational-emotive therapy of Ellis (1962) is being extended to the behavioral model (Goldfried, Decenteceo, & Weinberg, 1974). There has been greater attention in the literature to ecological concerns (Clark, Burgess, & Hendee, 1972), and a trend toward broad community/preventive programs (Stumphauzer, 1976; Stumphauzer, Aiken, & Veloz, in press). With rapid progress in this "electronic age," the electronic control of mind and behavior are fast becoming realities (Schwitzgebel & Schwitzgebel, 1973).

In the 1970's, behavior therapy is now widely taught to psychologists, psychiatrists, nonprofessionals, and increasingly, to teachers who are utilizing "token economies" and "engineered classrooms" with their students (O'Leary & O'Leary, 1972). Progress has been amply documented in working with the retarded (Neisworth & Smith, 1973). Behavior therapy has been utilized successfully with criminals and delinquents in institutions, clinics and in the community (Stumphauzer, 1973, 1976, in press).

Skinner's two recent books (1971, 1974) have further established a behavioral approach that modern man can take with his own destiny. Behavior modification has been popularized through such magazines as *Psychology Today,* in books for parents (Patterson, 1971b; Becker, 1971), in weight and smoking control centers, and in the "mass media" in general. It hasn't all been "good news," however. Some of the abuses of behavior therapy, especially in institutions, have been widely publicized with "bad press." Individually and collectively, behavior therapists are now looking at the issues facing them, and for that reason, we will now turn to a more detailed discussion of them. How these issues are dealt with will determine, in large part, the future course and success of behavior therapy.

ISSUES IN BEHAVIOR MODIFICATION

The ethical use of power is always a concern. The principles in this book are widely practiced today, and do have *powerful* effects. They work. The power of these principles, coupled with the *deliberateness* of their application, have led to many concerns, misunderstandings and issues. The principles themselves are passive tools; the issues really have to do with their *ethical* and *legal* applications.

Misuses and abuses of behavior modification receive wide, public attention. Further complications develop from attempts at legal regulation (Martin, 1975). The following is a list of issues facing practitioners of behavior modification in the 1970's, along with a brief discussion of each, and references to more detailed discourse elsewhere. These are "live" issues, and there is no intention to imply that they are settled at this time or that the list is complete.

1 / The Nature of Behavior Modification

One issue facing this area is the question of a clear delineation of the boundaries and nature of behavior modification. In what key ways is this therapy different from other therapies? In what ways similar? Bachrach (1965) and Eysenck (1959) have listed what they see as major similarities and differences between behavior therapy and psychodynamic therapy. Others do not see such clear differences (Marmor, 1971; Shectman, 1975).

Related to this is the issue, already mentioned, of "broad spectrum" vs. "scientific" behavior therapy (Lazarus, 1968; Wolpe, 1969, 1976b). Also, is there *one* behavior therapy or are there behavior therap*ies*? As noted in the history, modern behavior therapy sprang from at least three sources: the group in South Africa (Wolpe & Lazarus), the English group (Eysenck & Shapiro), and the American group (Skinner, his colleagues and students). To some extent they have developed quite different therapies, and their work has often appeared in separate journals, especially in the case of the Skinnerian approach and the *Journal of Applied Behavior Analysis.* Still, all are called behavioral.

Recently, Wolpe (1976a, 1976b) has critically explored what he considers the misunderstandings of this field by five categories of "malcontents":

1. those who deny the very foundations of behavior modification;
2. those who want a merger with psychoanalysis;
3. those who advocate "multimodal" techniques;
4. those who see behavior therapy entirely as cognitive change; and,
5. those who see it as simply an "exposure" technology.

2 / Manipulation and Control

This issue is a concern, often voiced, that behavior modification relies on certain people in power manipulating and controlling others, and that such manipulation is bad in a moral or ethical sense. Skinner (1953, 1971, 1974) has repeatedly pointed out that manipulation and control are already inherent aspects of the human condition, however subtle (e.g., in child rearing, in education, in our political system, etc.). Birk et al. (1973) succinctly conclude, with regard to psychotherapy, that effective "therapy with manipulation is a mirage that disappears on close scrutiny" (p. 46). Such control and manipulation, although already inherent in our society, are often applied haphazardly with unmeasured or unpredictable results. In behavior modification, the application of control is quite direct and intentional with effects that are (by intent) public. It is this aspect – the clear, effective, *deliberate* use of control – which seems to raise eyebrows.

Who should be the "controller"? This related question can be answered by stating that our social and political system has already and will continue to assign control and responsibility (i.e., to parents, to teachers, to law enforcers, and to individuals with regard to their own behavior). As Smith (1973) points out, behavior modification programs often begin with a relatively high degree of external control, but evolve toward the individual controlling his or her own environment and behavior. Indeed, in recent years, behavioral self-control has developed as a major behavior modification trend (see Chapter 20; Watson & Tharp, 1972; Bishop, 1973; Thorensen & Mahoney, 1974).

3 / Informed Consent

This is an issue facing all treatments and therapies, and behavior modification is no exception. A civil liberties issue, it is usually stated that patients have a legal right to be "fully informed" about the procedures and risks involved in the treatment being offered, and, in addition, that they be free to agree to, or to turn down the treatment after being so informed. Informed consent remains an issue, and a code of ethics for behavior therapy will likely encourage such practice (Braun, 1975).

4 / Aversion Procedures and Punishment

This is an especially complicated issue behavior therapists face. Techniques which utilize painful stimuli have been criticized on ethical and legal grounds as both immoral and "cruel and unusual punishment." Such procedures are especially open to criticism with "captive" patients, prisoners, and students as will be discussed later. While research indicates that such procedures do work, this research does not determine ethical decisions as to when they should be used.

Punishment and negative reinforcement have been two of the few procedures effective in stopping self-destructive head-banging in children, and in developing initial social contact with autistic children (Lovaas, Schaeffer, & Simmons, 1965). One may raise this disturbing question: Is it ethical or humane *not* to alleviate such severe problems when effective methods are known? Isn't our law enforcement and correctional system already entirely based on punishment *without* consent (Brady, 1974)?

The trend in behavior modification is toward positive controls of behavior (Stumphauzer, 1973, 1976, in press). When punishment is used it is often to stop a behavior, and in conjunction, positive controls are implemented to develop desirable, incompatible behavior (see Chapter 12). Informed consent would alleviate many of the concerns with aversive techniques, as would using them only as a last resort or in combination with other, positive means for developing adaptive behavior. At least one state (Minnesota) has already developed regulation of behavior modification in its state hospitals and has, in effect, excluded aversive reinforcement programs entirely (Lucero, Vail, & Scherber, 1968). Further confusing this issue is a mass media misrepresentation of these methods (e.g., Stanley Kubrick's film, *A Clockwork Orange*).

5 / Captive Patients, Captive Students, Captive Prisoners

This issue deals with the application of behavior modification methods to "captive" groups. "Captive" groups mean groups of people who are coerced into taking part in programs by various legal and quasi-legal means. Buehler (1973) differentiated these "closed" social systems from "open" social systems in which membership is voluntary. Again, the issue encompasses more than behavior modification alone. While these issues usually are aired with regard to the "rights of patients" and the "rights of prisoners," there is also a concern for the "rights of students" (Lee & Jacobs, 1973).

One criticism of behavior therapy in hospitals, prisons and schools is that there is treatment without consent and treatment through coercion. Such critics, however, fail to recognize that there is already coercion and lack of consent inherent in virtually all traditional institutional programs. There is serious question whether there can even be such a thing as voluntary consent in a closed setting (Schwitzgebel, 1971; Buehler, 1973; Brady, 1974). While the explicit communication may be "you are free to take part in this program if you wish," the implicit message may be an understood, "or else!" It seems that while the issue of forcing programs on patients, prisoners and students is a broad one, behavior modification is singled out because its methods are deliberate and its results public. Thus, criticism is directed at one particularly effective method that openly and deliberately accomplishes the implicit intention of institutional programs (i.e., education and behavior improvement).

6 / Conflict with Humanism

Another issue is that humanism and behavior modification are necessarily in conflict or are incompatible. Smith (1973) addressed herself directly to this issue, and one by one laid the fallacies of this argument to rest. First, control as utilized in behavior modification is not harmful or inhumane. Is it humane *not* to use a method that can stop suffering? Second, control is not always from external sources, but rather self-control is often both a method and a goal. Third, while behavior modification has been singled out for maintaining the "status quo" in school systems, for example, this is no more the case than with any effective educational method. Fourth, behavior therapists' interest in measurement, accurate appraisals of cause and effect and evaluation of progress is mistaken for being "mechanistic." Measuring behavior is simply a tool to gauge effectiveness, and can be consistent with the humanistic goals of "self-awareness" and "actualization."

7 / Certification

Who is to practice behavior modification and therapy? At issue is the question of whether any attempt should be made to certify those that some group feels are "qualified." Behavior modification principles are now widely applied in schools, hospitals and the community; the practitioners range from highly trained (in behavior modification) professionals to virtually untrained people who have attended a weekend "workshop" (Stein, 1975). From the beginning, however, behaviorists were quick to train nonprofessionals to modify behavior (Ayllon & Michael, 1959; Wahler, Winkel, Peterson, & Morrison, 1965) because:

1. wide-scale application was seen as both possible and desirable; and,
2. nonprofessionals (e.g., parents and teachers) were viewed as the *natural mediators* of behavior – they *are* the environment which teaches and changes behavior.

But people began to call themselves "Behavior Therapists," and with growing concern over abuses and the very nature of behavior therapy, the two professional associations began examining the desirability of certifying professional practitioners. The two do not seem to agree. While the Behavior Therapy and Research Society has published a "roster of clinical fellows" (*Journal of Behavior Therapy and Experimental Psychiatry,* 1973), the Association for Advancement of Behavior Therapy has been more cautious. The Association has been debating certification's pros (Cautela, 1975) and cons (Stuart, 1975a), and has polled its members. Results suggest that a majority are *against* certification as proposed (Stuart, 1975b). Some kind of regulation "from within" does seem likely, perhaps through certification at a later time, or perhaps by the development of a strict code of ethics.

8 / A Code of Ethics

Most of the issues already covered have to do with the ethical practice of behavior modification. Some feel that a clearly formulated "code of ethics" is needed. Braun (1975) outlined arguments for and against developing a code of ethics for behavior therapy.

One argument in favor of a code of ethics is a philosophical argument that a code of ethics is necessary to protect the rights of individuals. A second argument suggests that an organized, professional group needs a code of ethics to refer to as a standard. A third (legal) argument favors the development of a code of ethics because if behavior therapists don't develop one, the legal profession will force it through court suits and legislation.

Arguments, reviewed by Braun (1975), opposing such a code of ethics, see it as unnecessary and/or impractical. One such position states that behavior therapists do not need to defend themselves, they have done nothing wrong. Another counter argument is that the problems have been the result of an unenlightened public; and, again, we should not be forced into a binding code by those who do not really fully understand the approach.

Other arguments against developing a code are that it is too complex to regulate legislatively, that we are not ready for such a code at this time, and finally, that the responsibility for such a code cannot be assigned to any specific organization. As Braun (1975) concludes, behavior therapists will need to be prepared to take a recognizable posture on the ethical practice of behavior modification. Again, if behavior therapists don't regulate themselves and the training of others in this approach, then regulation will necessarily come from elsewhere – as a result of social and legal pressure.

HOW TO USE THIS BOOK

Behavior modification is the systematic application of *principles* of learning that have been developed through years of basic psychological research and practice. These principles are the very building blocks of *all* behavior change. Further, this is a rapidly growing field, and new developments are continually building on the foundation of the principles presented here. For that reason, there are no limited number of principles of behavior modification. The list of principles and techniques will grow and change with experience and careful research. The principles have not been fully applied and investigated; herein lies challenge for the new student and practitioner of behavior therapy.

There are four sections to this book. The first three chapters introduce basic concepts common to all behavior modification. Chapters 4 through 11 teach principles which *increase* behavior, while chapters in the third section, Chapters 12 to 17, show which principles are used to *decrease* behavior. Finally, Chapters 18 to 22 outline other additional principles. Some of the principles presented here are basic *principles of learning* that are applied directly in behavior modification (e.g., Principle of Positive Reinforcement). They are as close to "laws of behavior" as we have. Others are *hybrid principles*, techniques based on other principles of learning such as the Principle of Social Reinforcement. Still others are basic to almost every behavior therapy program (e.g., Principle of Behavior Measurement). The reader should not get the impression that the principles are all used equally; some are used frequently, others relatively rarely.

Also, you should not get the idea that these principles only function to change deviant behavior. They are principles that describe how we all learn *normal as well as abnormal* behavior. They are at work in shaping child behavior into adult behavior, in controlling how we learn and do our jobs, and are at work in how we behave socially. Look for them and their influence in your behavior and in the behavior of those around you. They are there.

The plan of this book is to teach these principles in three ways to maximize understanding and active student participation while learning:

1. to present a statement of the principle as clearly as possible with *programmed instruction;*
2. to *model* how others have applied each principle, both with children and adults; and,
3. to actively involve the reader in *practicing* the use of each principle.

1 / Programmed Instruction

At the beginning of each chapter a statement of the principle of behavior therapy is presented in as clear a manner as possible. It is the key to that chapter and also may be considered a summary statement. While you may not understand it completely on first reading, the goal of the remainder of the chapter is to see that you do.

Immediately following the statement of the principle is a program to teach that principle. This program was developed following Evans's (1961) five points of programmed instruction. First, is the use of small steps of learning for the maximizing of student success. Second, is active responding by the student by writing in answers. Third, is immediate confirmation by providing answers on the page. Fourth, is self-pacing with students going through each chapter at their own particular pace. And fifth, is program testing, which was used in the development of the program by revising sections after receiving reader and student feedback. This program has been used in training programs, with various levels of students, and revised over the last two years (Burkhart, Behles, & Stumphauzer, 1976; Teicher, Sinay, & Stumphauzer, 1976).

First, read the principle over several times until it is fairly clear. Next, do the program for that principle. It is necessary to *write* in the words that should go in the blanks; you will learn more if you do. The first letter of each word is given. Check your answer with the word given at the end of the program (immediate confirmation). If it is right, you have learned it! If it is wrong, change it to the right answer. Get involved in the program. Underline important parts, write notes or ideas in the margin. Now read the principle again to see that you thoroughly understand it.

2 / Modeling

Another effective way of learning is to observe how others have done something. We learn a great deal by example (see Chapter 19). This is no less true in this field. If we can see how others have applied one of the principles, it makes it much more clear and alive. For this reason two studies or cases were chosen as models or examples of each principle for the reader. All of the principles have been applied with children and adults, and for this reason one example of each is given. You can see how programs vary with different age groups and populations. The principles stay the same.

These particular models were selected for several reasons. The most important selection criterion was that the study or case clearly demonstrate that particular principle. Next, the goal was to select only articles published in journals that are available in most college libraries so that instructors or students interested in a particular study could read the full report. Articles were *not* selected for their particular scientific rigor, and, in fact, many are simply case presentations. Many of them are, however, "classics" in the behavior modification literature.

The summaries presented here are necessarily limited; they don't go into detail or show all aspects of each case. Their goal is simply to clearly model the application of each principle, no more. The author(s), title and source are given for each, together with the behavior under study, and a short statement of the program. First, read each example or model of how others have applied that principle with both children and adults, and fill in the blanks. Read both examples even though you may work exclusively with either children or adults. Look especially at which behavior was the focus of the study and how it was measured, how *the researchers* used that principle, and what behavior change resulted. The brief program at the end of each example again requires student responding, gives immediate confirmation, and summarizes how *that* principle was applied in *that* program.

3 / Practice

While both responding to programmed instruction and observing how others use principles are effective in learning behavior modification, it is only when you practice applying these principles yourself that you will see how they could work in your particular program or treatment situation. This is when they become real for you.

At the end of each chapter is a *Practice Page* for you to take each principle and design a brief plan to apply that principle in your own work. First, there is a space for *Behavior to Be Changed.* Get very specific. A rule might be to select behaviors that are *of concern* and that are *observable* or *countable* (see Chapter 3). Select behaviors carefully. While you may know what you mean by "hyperactive," it is not very easy to measure, and many would not agree on whether or not it occurred. Perhaps "number of times he leaves seat" would be better. That *can* be counted, and two people watching would agree. "Number of times cries" and "number of times talks about suicide" would be better than "depressed."

The second space is for *How this Behavior Could Be Measured.* Decide, ahead of time, on how it will be measured. Try measuring it! Would it be counted? By whom? When? How will it be recorded or kept track of? This is more than an exercise. It will make the importance (and one of the key attributes) of behavior modification stand out for you. You will learn to choose behaviors that *are* measurable. Measurement is that important, as you will see in Chapter 3. The author has developed a Daily Behavior Graph (Stumphauzer, 1972) which allows day-by-day recording and graphing of behaviors, and a Daily Behavior Card (Stumphauzer, 1974a) for a daily recording of behaviors on a portable 3 x 5 card which can be carried by students, patients, or others. Another method for keeping track of your daily behavior is the wrist counter.

Next, use the *Practice Page* to plan how you could apply each principle in your own work. In the *Behavioral Plan* section write down your own plan for applying *that* principle to change *that* particular behavior you listed. Spell it out point by point, making it as realistic as possible. This is your chance to put what you have learned (from the program and the models) to work for you.

In the fourth space, *Possible Ethical and Legal Issues,* note the issues that might or *should* come up in carrying through the behavioral plan you have outlined. Review the general issues discussed earlier in the Introduction. While you obviously won't know all the ethical or legal repercussions of a behavior modification plan, write down the ones you can think of. Ask others. This is a good section for discussion with other students, teachers or therapists. As noted earlier, behavior modifiers are increasingly involved in considering ethical and legal issues. The new student of this field would do well to consider these issues from the start – right here on the *Practice Page* and in discussion. (See Figures 1 and 2.)

The book is designed to first teach you the principles of behavior therapy, to show you how others have used these principles to change behavior, and finally, to get you to consider how you might apply these principles yourself in *your* daily work.

While several principles are taught in this book, they will not be equally useful for all of you. Teachers will be interested in certain basic principles, while psychotherapists may be interested in other, clinical techniques. As you have seen in an earlier section, many ethical and legal issues are involved, especially in applying principles which utilize painful stimuli. However, any serious student of behavior therapy should be familiar with these principles and should complete all chapters.

Notice that the plan on the *Practice Page* is tentative – how you *might* apply each principle. Experience and ability will vary with each student-reader. In some cases, of course, you will be able to apply the principles immediately. You could, for example, use social reinforcement to increase desirable behavior in a student or patient. Other principles, such as aversion therapy, are much more complex and are used only by highly qualified professionals and often by them in very special circumstances. To learn more, you may want to look at some of your own behavior first; say, a habit like smoking, or a problem area like not completing projects. This might be a good place to start to get experience measuring and changing behavior.

If a principle and an example seem particularly applicable to your program or to a particular person you are working with, it is suggested you go to the original work and read it thoroughly. Then you should seek help or supervision from a qualified behavior therapist. Consultants are available to most school systems, hospitals, probation departments and community projects. Psychologists and some

Figure 1.

Example of a Practice Page from a Community Worker*

PRACTICE PAGE

This is the way that I might use the Principle of Modeling and Imitation:

1. BEHAVIOR TO BE CHANGED:

   Excessive ***wine drinking*** *in a 14-year-old Chicano.*

2. HOW THIS BEHAVIOR COULD BE MEASURED:

   a. Observe and record "been drinking" or "not been drinking" at counseling center, home, school and "hang out."

   b. Encourage self-measurement of drinking on Daily Behavior Card.

3. BEHAVIORAL PLAN (How I might use *modeling* and *imitation* to change *this* behavior):

   a. Expose him to as many ***non****-drinking models as possible, yet, people he would like to be with (similar age, social status, etc.).*

   b. Reinforce imitation of non-drinking behavior (alternate "legal highs" like sports, helping others, getting job, etc.).

4. POSSIBLE ETHICAL AND LEGAL ISSUES:

   a. It is illegal for him to buy or have wine.

   b. When we begin measuring drinking will this change the way school and parents act toward him?

   c. Drinking is ***highly*** *valued by his peer group. What effect will* ***stopping*** *have?*

---

*Teicher, J.D., Sinay, R.D., & Stumphauzer, J.S. Training community-based paraprofessionals as behavior therapists with families of alcohol abusing adolescents. *American Journal of Psychiatry,* 1976, 133, 847-850.

Figure 2.

Example of a Practice Page from a Probation Officer*

PRACTICE PAGE

This is the way that I might use the Principle of Negative Reinforcement:

1. BEHAVIOR TO BE CHANGED:

   Attending school *(is on probation for truancy and theft).*

2. HOW THIS BEHAVIOR COULD BE MEASURED:

   Get a weekly ***attendance report*** *from school.*

3. BEHAVIORAL PLAN (How I might use *negative reinforcement* to change *this* behavior):

   For every full week of school attendance he can get one week off of probation period (attending school will terminate the aversive probation).

4. POSSIBLE ETHICAL AND LEGAL ISSUES:

   Will the court go along with this? Has been done in adult division.

---

*Burkhart, B.R., Behles, M.W., & Stumphauzer, J.S. Training juvenile probation officers in behavior modification: Knowledge, attitude change, or behavioral competence? *Behavior Therapy,* 1976, 7, 47-53.

psychiatrists are often especially trained to do behavior modification training and consultation.

As discussed in the earlier section on issues, there is, as yet, no strict regulation or certification of behavior therapists. However, the practice of professions such as psychology and psychiatry do usually require state licensing. If a particular topic interests you, you should do more reading about it in books and the journals mentioned earlier. Also, you are encouraged to participate in the growing number of local and regional conferences or workshops on behavior therapy and modification. They provide a good opportunity to see what people are doing in this area. You will usually find a display of books and equipment, and often have the opportunity to take an active part in training workshops.

Finally, in learning the principles of behavior therapy, let us consider how these principles can be used in helping you learn and apply the principles themselves. Think of and try ways that you can reward or reinforce yourself for completing chapters of the book. Reward yourself! Find things or activities or people that could be available to you *after* you complete sections and learn more. Work on improving some of your own habits or behaviors. Discuss the things you learn with others, or even better, work your way through it with someone you enjoy. See the chapter on "Self-Control" for more ideas.

You could just read this book and probably learn about behavior modification, but only when you get actively involved will you make the most of the opportunity. This program can teach you the principles so that you can understand them, and can provide models for how others have used these principles. But only when *you* design a behavior modification plan and see how these principles could work to change behavior that is important to you, will you really learn their importance and applications.

Chapter 2

Principle of Behavioral Analysis

CAUSES **AND POTENTIAL** ***CONTROLS*** **OF PROBLEM BEHAVIORS MAY BE OBJECTIVELY IDENTIFIED AND THEN UTILIZED IN TREATMENT.**

Behavior is carefully analyzed in a behavioral (1) a______________. In behavior therapy, behavioral analysis takes the place of the traditional diagnostic process. An objective assessment is made of both behaviors and the stimuli that control them. Problem (2) b____________ are listed and specified. Non-problem behaviors are also specified. How could the good behaviors be expanded or rewarded more?

Stimuli or events that set off or lead up to problem behaviors are investigated because these (3) s______________ or events may be part of the cause of the problem. If this is so, altering or stopping these stimuli or events may alter or stop the problem (4) b____________. If arguments often lead to overeating, then stopping (5) a____________ may stop the excessive eating.

What happens right after problem behaviors occur is also investigated. The results or *consequences* of problem behaviors are also a cause of the behavior. Changing or stopping the consequences of a particular behavior may change or stop the behavior. If a child's tantrums result in a lot of attention, then stopping that (6) a____________ may stop the (7) t______________.

An analysis of what are strong motivations, strong rewards and punishments, is usually done to determine both if they are currently controlling behavior, and if they potentially could be used to change or (8) c______________ behavior. If a child wants a bicycle more than anything then a (9) b____________ may be what he could earn in the treatment program.

Problem behaviors, non-problem behaviors, stimuli, rewards and punishments are all examined in light of the general social and cultural system the individual is living in. This behavioral (10) a____________ then leads logically to suggestions of what changes in the environment will lead to changes in (11) b______________, to less problematic living.

1. analysis	5. arguments	9. bicycle
2. behaviors	6. attention	10. analysis
3. stimuli	7. tantrums	11. behavior
4. behaviors	8. control	

EXAMPLE OF BEHAVIORAL ANALYSIS WITH CHILDREN

Authors: Buehler, R.E., Patterson, G.R., & Furniss, J.M.
Title: The reinforcement of behavior in institutional settings.
Source: *Behaviour Research and Therapy,* 1966, 4, 157-167.
Behavior: Antisocial and pro-social behavior.
Analysis: Analysis of consequences: Some "causes" of delinquent behavior.

In a classic study, these investigators conducted a behavioral analysis in schools for delinquent girls. Observers in the schools kept records of the girls' behavior, which was classified as pro-social or antisocial. Further, what happened right after the behaviors (the consequences) were recorded as well. The reactions (consequences) of peers and the consequences provided by staff were noted separately. This careful behavioral analysis revealed that peers consistently rewarded antisocial behavior, while staff were inconsistent both in punishing such antisocial behavior, and in rewarding good behavior. In brief, the analysis showed that the school was teaching delinquent behavior! This behavioral analysis would suggest that in order for the schools to promote pro-social behavior, peer rewards for bad behavior would have to be (1) s________________, and that staff would have to more consistently (2) r________________ good behavior and punish (3) a________________, or delinquent behavior.

1. stopped 2. reward 3. antisocial

EXAMPLE OF BEHAVIORAL ANALYSIS WITH ADULTS

Authors: Cautela, J.R., & Kastenbaum, R.

Title: A reinforcement survey schedule for use in therapy, training and research.

Source: *Psychological Reports,* 1967, 20, 1115-1130.

Behavior: Rating reinforcers.

Analysis: Survey of rewards or reinforcers: Determining "controls" of behavior.

In a behavioral analysis it is often necessary to determine the strongest motivations in a person's life, i.e., what the strongest rewards or reinforcers available are. In this paper, Cautela and Kastenbaum provide a useful adult reinforcement survey form which clients are asked to fill out. There is a long list of things and activities, and the client is to rate each one with regard to "how much pleasure it gives you nowadays." The behavior therapist and the client can then use this information to decide which rewards or (1) r____________ would be reasonable to use in the (2) t____________ program. Things or activities rated as most pleasurable would be the (3) m____________ effective rewards for teaching or changing behavior.

1. reinforcers 2. treatment 3. most

PRACTICE PAGE

This is the way that I might use the Principle of Behavioral Analysis:

1. BEHAVIOR TO BE CHANGED:

2. HOW THIS BEHAVIOR COULD BE MEASURED:

3. BEHAVIORAL PLAN (How I might use *behavioral analysis* to understand *this* behavior):

4. POSSIBLE ETHICAL AND LEGAL ISSUES:

I've finished my list of reinforcers!

Chapter 3

Principle of Behavior Measurement

EFFECTIVE BEHAVIOR MEASUREMENT DEPENDS UPON SYSTEMATIC RECORDING OF BEHAVIOR WHICH IS *OBSERVABLE, COUNTABLE* AND *CAN BE AGREED UPON.*

One cornerstone of behavior therapy is the careful selection and measurement of behavior. First of all, we must select behaviors that are important (that we wish to change) and behaviors that are observable (that we can see, count and agree on). "Number of tantrums" and "number of words spoken" are good examples of (1) o__________ behaviors. We can (2) s__________ or hear them, we can (3) c__________ the number of times they occur, and we can usually (4) a__________ on whether they happened or not. "Depressed" and "being good" are more complicated behaviors which we often don't agree on. It is usually better to break them down into more simple, (5) o__________ behaviors like "cried," "talked about suicide," or "asked to go out," and "came home on time."

In behavior therapy we measure behavior first to see how often it occurs *before* we do anything to change it, and this is called the "baseline" of the behavior. This (6) b__________ tells us how extensive the problem behavior is, and the (7) b__________ also gives us a standard to compare progress with, after we begin a behavioral program. If there is a change from baseline, a measurable improvement, then we are making progress. If there is no (8) c__________ from baseline, then we need to adjust the program until there is.

(9) M__________ of behavior and comparisons to (10) b__________ are very important because they give us feedback and a kind of progress report.

There are many ways to measure behavior, and it should be measured often. You or someone else close to the person can simply keep a daily total of the (11) n__________ of times the behavior happens, or the frequency. This can be done on a wrist golf score counter, on paper, a bulletin board, or 3 x 5 cards. Behavior (12) m__________ is always an important part of a behavioral program, and without it you will not know if your program is working.

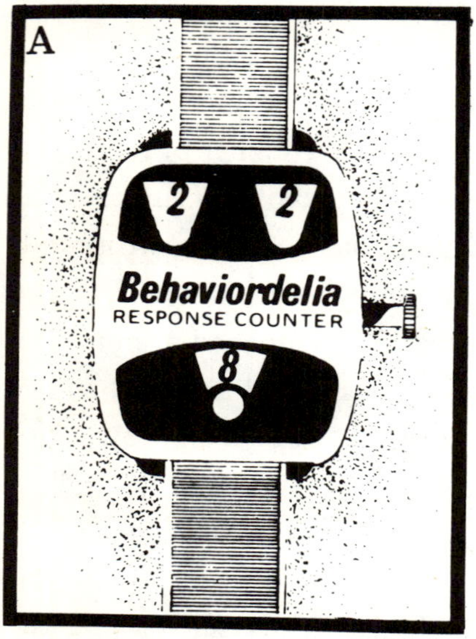

THE DIAL COUNTER

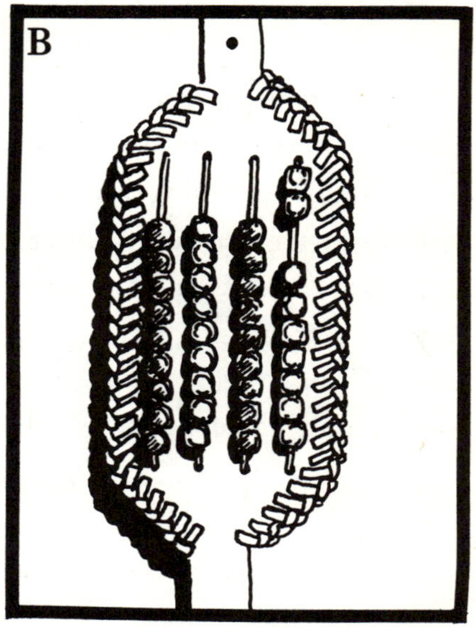

THE BEAD COUNTER

These response counters are available from BEHAVIORDELIA, INC.

DBC DAILY BEHAVIOR CARD

Name Charlie   Date 12/20

BEHAVIORS:	M*	T	W	T	F	S	S	Signatures:
1 Spoketo Staff	1	1	2	2	2	2	1	J. Thomas
2. Talk to self	3	3	1	1	0	1	0	J. Thomas
3. # Tantrums	1	2	0	0	0	1	0	J. Thomas
4. Dressed by 8:15	0	0	1	1	1	1	1	J. Thomas
Totals:	5	6	4	3	3	4	3	28

*frenquency, points, check, or rating:
3=very frequently   2=often
1=occassionaly   0=never

Daily Behavior Graph

NAME: CHARLIE

MONTH: DECEMBER

day:	Mon.	Tues.	Wed.	Thurs.	Fri.	Sat.	Sun.
date	14	15	16	17	18	19	20

BEHAVIOR ONE: SPOKE TO STAFF (3, 2, 1, 0)

BEHAVIOR TWO: TALKING + SMILING TO HIMSELF (3, 2, 1, 0)

BEHAVIOR THREE: NUMBER OF TANTRUMS (3, 2, 1, 0)

BEHAVIOR FOUR: UP + DRESSED BY 8:15 (YES ~~3~~, ~~2~~, ~~1~~, NO ~~0~~)

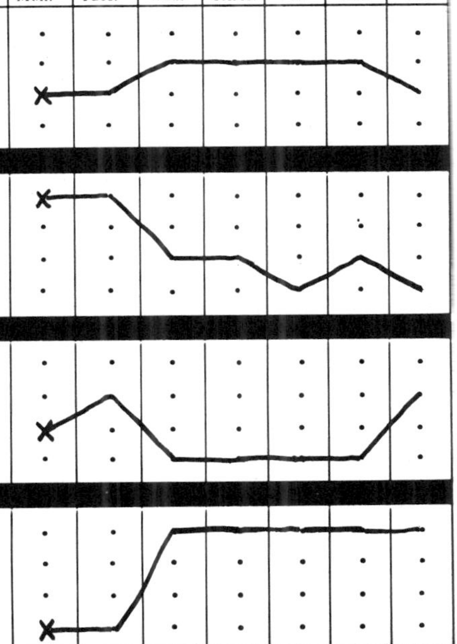

Observer's signature, time and special circumstances of rating each day:

Mon.	Tues.	Wed.	Thurs.	Fri.	Sat.	Sun.
J.T. 8:00 PM	J.T. 7:00 PM *BEGIN NEW BEHAVIOR PROGRAM	J.T. 8:00 PM	J.T. 7:30 PM	J.T. 8:00 PM	J.T. 7:00 PM *Increase in medication.	J.T. 7:30 PM

FOR RATING:
3 = Very frequently
2 = Often
1 = Occasionally
0 = Never

Remember, choose simple (13) b____________ that are (14) o____________, that you or someone can (15) s____________, can (16) c____________, and can (17) a____________ on whether or not they happened. The (18) b____________ is the level of the behavior before changing anything. It tells us how serious the problem is, and later, whether our program is working or not.

1. observable
2. see
3. count
4. agree
5. observable
6. baseline
7. baseline
8. change
9. measurement
10. baseline
11. number
12. measurement
13. behaviors
14. observable
15. see
16. count
17. agree
18. baseline

EXAMPLE OF MEASUREMENT WITH CHILDREN

Authors: Bailey, J.S., Wolf, M.M., & Phillips, E.L.
Title: Home-based reinforcement and the modification of predelinquents' classroom behavior.
Source: *Journal of Applied Behavior Analysis,* 1970, 3, 223-233.
Behaviors: "Studied whole period" and "obeyed class rules."
Measurement: Teacher checking yes or no on daily 4 x 5 card.

Measuring behavior *in school* is fairly difficult for teachers and nearly impossible for parents. Traditional report cards are too general and too delayed to be effective behavior measurement for parents to use in improving the school behavior of their youngsters. These authors took an obvious, yet innovative step of sending a simple 4 x 5 card to school with several predelinquents from a group home called

Achievement Place. The card had a space labeled "studied whole period" and another labeled "obeyed the class rules." The teachers then checked either yes or no. Behavior *at school,* as measured on the card, then determined the number of points the youngsters could earn *at home,* and school behavior was improved in this way. Here, teachers measured behavior effectively for parents by writing yes or no for (1) "s__________ whole period" and (2) "o__________ class rules" on a daily 4 x 5 (3) c__________.

1. studied 2. obeyed 3. card

EXAMPLE OF MEASUREMENT WITH ADULTS

Author: Maletzky, B.M.

Title: Behavior recording as treatment: A brief note.

Source: *Behavior Therapy,* 1974, 5, 107-111.

Behaviors: Scratching, fingernail biting, hand raising, tics, out of seat.

Measurement: Frequency counts on a wrist counter.

Simply measuring or counting a behavior may change it. In the five cases presented in this paper, the person with a problem behavior was asked to measure or count it on a cumulative wrist counter, and to record it on graph paper daily. Maletzky showed that this kind of self-counting did decrease the number of times problem behaviors occurred.

In one case, for example, a woman who was a life-long fingernail biter was asked to count this behavior on her wrist counter. Nail biting declined over the eight weeks that she wore it, but increased when she stopped wearing it. Later she wore the counter one week of every four which kept the rate of nail biting down. One reason simply measuring a behavior changes it is that careful attention is then directed at the behavior and this may be seen as punishment. Or, there may be an expectancy to change. One person said she was more aware of *not* scratching when she felt the counter on her wrist. A behavior may level off after behavior measurement is started, and then a behavioral intervention could be tried. In this study, however, simply (1) c______________ behaviors on a (2) w______________ counter did change the frequency of the behaviors.

1. counting 2. wrist

PRACTICE PAGE

This is the way that I might use the Principle of Behavior Measurement:

1. BEHAVIOR TO BE CHANGED:

2. HOW THIS BEHAVIOR COULD BE MEASURED:

3. BEHAVIORAL PLAN (How I might use *behavior measurement* to understand *this* behavior):

4. POSSIBLE ETHICAL AND LEGAL ISSUES:

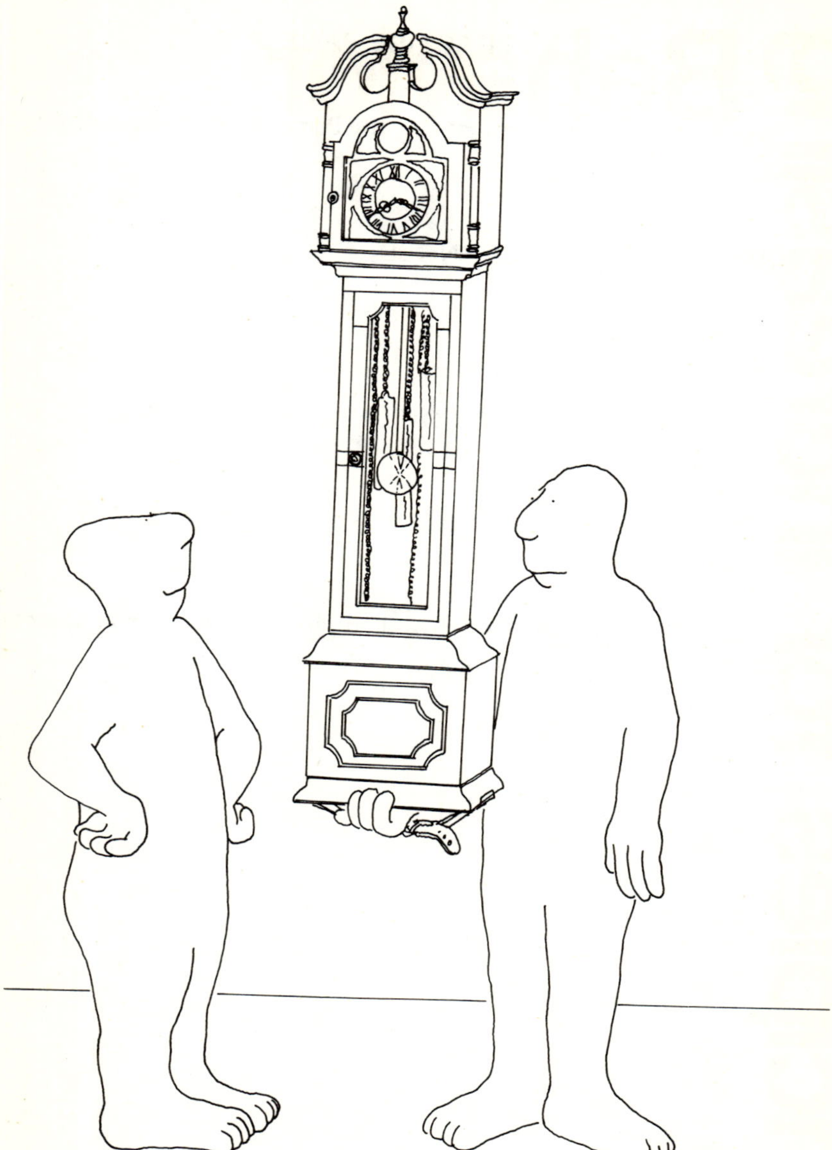

When you told me you had a new wrist counter . . .

Principles for Increasing Behavior

Chapter 4

Principle of Positive Reinforcement

IF A CONSEQUENCE OR RESULT OF A BEHAVIOR HAS THE EFFECT OF *INCREASING* THE STRENGTH OR FREQUENCY OF THAT BEHAVIOR, THEN *POSITIVE REINFORCEMENT* HAS TAKEN PLACE.

A consequence is a result or outcome of a behavior. A behavior occurs, and the result of that behavior is called a (1) c________________. The consequence is positive (2) r________________ if its occurrence has the effect of increasing the behavior that it follows. A (3) p________________ r________________ increases behavior.

If a child says "please" when he wants a cookie, and his mother gives him the cookie, his behavior is saying (4) "p________________," and the cookie that his mother gives him is a (5) p________________ r________________. We should expect the boy to say (6) "p________________" more often because he has been (7) p________________ r________________ for that behavior.

It is important to note that (8) p________________ r________________ is most effective if it *immediately* follows the behavior. The outcome or result of a behavior is called a (9) c________________. When its occurrence has the effect of increasing the behavior that it follows it is a (10) p________________ r________________. It is best when it (11) i________________ follows the behavior.

---

1. consequence
2. reinforcement
3. positive reinforcer
4. please
5. positive reinforcer
6. please
7. positively reinforced
8. positive reinforcement
9. consequence
10. positive reinforcer
11. immediately

EXAMPLE OF POSITIVE REINFORCEMENT WITH CHILDREN

Authors: Azrin, N.H., & Lindsley, O.R.

Title: The reinforcement of cooperation between children.

Source: *Journal of Abnormal and Social Psychology,* 1956, 52, 100-102.

Behavior: Social cooperation.

Positive Reinforcement: Candy.

There is probably nothing more basic to people living together than social cooperation, or doing things together. As children grow, they must gradually learn to live and work together with others. This is the basis of socialization as we know it. Many of the clinical problems we see are instances of failure to learn cooperation: the child who fights with his siblings; the child who does not get along in school. In this brilliant and often cited study, Azrin and Lindsley first developed a simple cooperative task, and then went about systematically modifying the behavior with positive reinforcement. While they reduced cooperation to perhaps its simplest form, their design can and has been easily extended to complex cooperative behavior.

Each of 10 pairs of children was asked to play a game. Each player was seated at a table fitted with a stylus and three holes on each side. They were told that some of the time jelly beans would drop into the cup. Positive reinforcement (jelly beans) immediately followed cooperation (here, each putting his stylus into the corresponding hole opposite his partner's). All 10 teams learned this cooperative behavior within 10 minutes. Leader/follower relationships developed as did sharing behavior. In two cases the researchers first observed one child taking all, the second child refusing to cooperate. Finally verbal agreements on sharing the candy led to cooperation. (1) C____________ was learned through the application of positive reinforcement. Jelly beans (the reinforcers) were contingent on cooperation. Cooperation increased following (2) p____________ r____________.

1. cooperation 2. positive reinforcement

EXAMPLE OF POSITIVE REINFORCEMENT WITH ADULTS

Author: Stumphauzer, J.S.

Title: Application of reinforcement contingencies with a 23-year-old anorexic patient.

Source: *Psychological Reports,* 1969, 24, 109-110.

Behavior: Eating.

Positive Reinforcement: Home passes.

Stopping their normal eating behavior is a common behavior in many hospitalized psychiatric patients, both children and adults. In severe cases (e.g., anorexia nervosa) rapid intervention is often required to sustain life. In this case a 23-year-old male was admitted to a psychiatric hospital after threatening suicide and refusing to eat for several days. He was diagnosed anorexia nervosa. He was uncooperative on the ward and was steadily losing weight.

Ward staff noted that the only thing he did seem interested in was seeing his uncle. At that time home passes were implemented as positive reinforcement for cooperation and eating. Specifically, the first contingency was, "if you cooperate with the ward staff and eat regular meals today, you can go on a three-hour pass with your uncle tomorrow." He remained uncooperative and was not reinforced. He was very disappointed, and was offered the same contingency again the next day. He did cooperate and eat for the next several days, went on passes, steadily gained weight and was discharged. In this case cooperation and (1) e______________ were reinforced with home passes. The passes worked as (2) p______________ r______________ because they acted to (3) i______________ cooperation and eating.

1. eating 2. positive reinforcers 3. increase

PRACTICE PAGE

This is the way that I might use the Principle of Positive Reinforcement:

1. BEHAVIOR TO BE CHANGED:

2. HOW THIS BEHAVIOR COULD BE MEASURED:

3. BEHAVIORAL PLAN (How I might use *positive reinforcement* to change *this* behavior):

4. POSSIBLE ETHICAL AND LEGAL ISSUES:

Chapter 5

Principle of Negative Reinforcement

IF THE *REMOVAL* OF AN *AVERSIVE* STIMULUS AS THE CONSEQUENCE OF A BEHAVIOR *INCREASES* THE STRENGTH OR FREQUENCY OF THAT BEHAVIOR, THEN *NEGATIVE REINFORCEMENT* HAS TAKEN PLACE.

Positive reinforcement increases the behavior that it follows. Negative reinforcement also *increases* the behavior that it follows. *Both* positive reinforcement and negative reinforcement (1) i__________ the strength or frequency of the behavior they follow.

The difference between positive reinforcement and (2) n__________ r__________ is that in positive reinforcement we use a positive stimulus to increase behavior, and in (3) n__________ r__________ we use the *termination* of an *aversive* stimulus to increase behavior. In other words, we stop something that is unpleasant so that a given behavior will increase. If a behavior (4) t__________ or stops an aversive stimulus the result will be an (5) i__________ in that behavior, and this process is called (6) n__________ r__________.

We learn a great many behaviors by doing something to stop or turn off aversive or uncomfortable stimulation. If a man is sitting in a hot room, he learns to do something about it. The hot, uncomfortable room is (7) a__________ to him. If he gets up and adjusts the thermostat this behavior turns off the aversive stimulus.

This is an example of (8) n__________ r__________ because the behavior of (9) a__________ the thermostat acts to terminate an uncomfortable or (10) a__________ situation. Because of this (11) n__________ r__________ we would expect the behavior of adjusting the thermostat when hot to occur more often when the person is in a hot room.

1. increase
2. negative reinforcement
3. negative reinforcement
4. terminates
5. increase
6. negative reinforcement
7. aversive
8. negative reinforcement
9. adjusting
10. aversive
11. negative reinforcement

EXAMPLE OF NEGATIVE REINFORCEMENT WITH CHILDREN

Authors: Lovaas, O.I., Schaeffer, B., & Simmons, J.Q.

Title: Building social behavior in autistic children by use of electric shock.

Source: *Journal of Experimental Research in Personality,* 1965, 1, 99-109.

Behavior: Autistic behavior.

Negative Reinforcement: Termination of electric shock.

Autistic children have striking behavioral deficits: they show no social responsiveness, speech or appropriate play with objects. In addition, they spend most of their time engaging in self-stimulatory behavior and making repetitive bodily movements. In this classic study, Lovaas, Schaeffer and Simmons established social behavior in autistic five-year-old twins by using negative reinforcement.

A special room with an electrified grid floor was used. Each child was barefoot, but the investigator wore shoes. The electrical current was turned on and the child was asked to "come here." If he didn't come, the child experienced pain until he went to the experimenter. When the child touched or hugged the investigator the shock was turned off. The *termination* of aversive stimulation contingent on this social approach behavior had the effect of *increasing* this and other social behavior (negative reinforcement). It is noteworthy that affection and other social behaviors toward adults increased after adults had been associated with shock reduction. (You should review the issue in the Introduction to this text regarding legal and ethical aspects of using pain to change behavior.) (1) S_______________ behavior increased in these autistic children when this kind of behavior was made contingent upon electric shock *termination* (2. n_______________ r_______________).

1. social 2. negative reinforcement

EXAMPLE OF NEGATIVE REINFORCEMENT WITH ADULTS

Authors: Azrin, N., Rubin, H., O'Brian, F., Ayllon, T., & Roll, D.
Title: Behavioral engineering: Postural control by a portable operant apparatus.
Source: *Journal of Applied Behavior Analysis,* 1968, 1, 99-108.
Behavior: Slouching.
Negative Reinforcement: Termination of aversive tone.

In this study the posture of several adults was controlled with the use of a special apparatus and a combination of punishment and negative reinforcement. A small apparatus was worn around the neck and upper body. In the event of slouching an aversive sound was emitted (punishment), and then an improvement in posture would result in *termination* of the aversive tone (negative reinforcement). Not slouching was reinforced then by the (1) t_______________ of the aversive sound, and we might expect not slouching or an increase in good posture. With this combination of punishment and (2) n_______________ r_______________, slouching did decrease for each person wearing the apparatus.

1. termination 2. negative reinforcement

PRACTICE PAGE

This is the way that I might use the Principle of Negative Reinforcement:

1. BEHAVIOR TO BE CHANGED:

2. HOW THIS BEHAVIOR COULD BE MEASURED:

3. BEHAVIORAL PLAN (How I might use *negative reinforcement* to change *this* behavior):

4. POSSIBLE LEGAL AND ETHICAL ISSUES:

Chapter 6

Principle of Shaping

DESIRABLE BEHAVIOR MAY BE *GRADUALLY* PRODUCED BY SELECTIVELY REINFORCING BEHAVIOR THAT *APPROXIMATES* IT.

When we want a person to develop a complicated behavior that he or she does not already know, we can gradually develop it or (1) s__________ it. Shaping is a (2) g__________ process of selectively reinforcing behavior that is closer and closer to the end goal behavior which we want. Shaping is the successive approximation of the behavior we're looking for.

Learning to talk is a very complicated learning process, both in normal children and in the retarded or severely disordered, and doesn't happen "all of a sudden." It usually is a very (3) g__________ learning process that includes (4) s__________. It may start with the child randomly babbling, and by our showing a lot of approval when he comes up with "da-da" or "ma-ma." We reinforce his utterings when they are closer and closer to the sounds in our language that we want him to learn; we (5) s__________ talking. Other processes are involved in such a complex behavior; but using attention or (6) r__________, and gradual (7) s__________ or (8) s__________ a__________ are of key importance.

---

1. shape
2. gradual
3. gradual
4. shaping
5. shape
6. reinforcement
7. shaping
8. successive approximation

EXAMPLE OF SHAPING WITH CHILDREN

Authors: Lovaas, O.I., Berberich, J., Perloff, B., & Schaeffer, B.
Title: Acquisition of imitative speech by schizophrenic children.
Source: *Science,* 1966, 162, 705-707.
Behavior: Speech.
Shaping: Reinforcing approximations to speech.

I realize it's the only thing he knows how to say,
but maybe you shouldn't be encouraging profanity.

With most children, speech develops without any particular problem, or, for that matter, without our understanding of how it is learned. Autistic or schizophrenic children show little speech development. These authors show in detail how they taught two mute schizophrenic six-year-old boys to talk. Reward (spoonful of child's meal), punishment (spanking, shouting), and very careful shaping were used.

In the first stage the children were reinforced for all vocalizations, and for looking at the adult's mouth. In the next phase, the adult made a sound and the child was reinforced if he made *any* vocal response within six seconds. In the third stage, there was an additional requirement that the child actually say what the adult had said. With this kind of gradual (1) s______________, the boys began to develop (2) s______________, and they were also learning to (3) i______________ adult behavior.

1. shaping 2. speech 3. imitate

EXAMPLE OF SHAPING WITH ADULTS

Authors: Ayllon, T., & Haughton, E.
Title: Control of the behavior of schizophrenic patients by food.
Source: *Journal of the Experimental Analysis of Behavior,* 1962, 5, 343-352.
Behavior: Cooperation.
Shaping: Gradual approximation of cooperative behavior.

In this series of classic studies, Ayllon and Haughton show the use of meals in controlling behavior of 45 chronic schizophrenics on a psychiatric ward. When the study first started, many of the patients did not eat, were spoon-fed, given a great deal of attention, etc. Later, access to the dining room was only possible when a coin was dropped into a slot. A cooperative behavior (two patients pushing two buttons at the same time to activate a buzzer) was required before meals, to get the coin. Verbal shaping was used by first telling the patients to push the button, and then that two had to push their buttons at the same time to make the buzzer go and to get the coins. The coin and then the meals served as (1) r________________. All patients learned the complicated chain of behaviors, but a gradual process of (2) s________________ was required at first.

---

1. reinforcement 2. shaping

PRACTICE PAGE

This is the way that I might use the Principle of Shaping:

1. BEHAVIOR TO BE SHAPED:

2. HOW THIS BEHAVIOR COULD BE MEASURED:

3. BEHAVIORAL PLAN (How I might use *shaping* to gradually produce *this* behavior):

4. POSSIBLE ETHICAL AND LEGAL ISSUES:

Chapter 7

Principle of Schedules of Reinforcement

THE FREQUENCY OF BEHAVIOR, THE PATTERN OF BEHAVIOR, AND RESISTANCE TO EXTINCTION ALL DEPEND UPON THE PARTICULAR *SCHEDULE* OF REINFORCEMENT USED.

How regular reinforcement is, or whether or not it occurs every single time the behavior occurs, does play a key role in teaching and maintaining behavior. Whether a behavior is reinforced every time or only once in a while, is what we call a (1) s______________ of reinforcement.

With continuous reinforcement the behavior is reinforced *every* time, or (2) c______________. This schedule is most effective in shaping new behavior or, initially, in getting a new behavior going. But you must remember that this (3) s______________ also results in rapid extinction (decrease in the behavior's frequency or strength) when reinforcement stops. If we were playing a slot machine and were winning every single time and suddenly we stopped winning, we would stop playing fairly quickly, or (4) e______________.

With intermittent reinforcement the behavior is not reinforced every time, but rather only once in a while, or (5) i______________. This kind of (6) s______________ is most effective in keeping a behavior going or (7) m______________ it over a long period of time. Extinction is slower with (8) i______________ reinforcement. This intermittent schedule is the one that keeps many behaviors going. It is why gamblers keep spending their money – because they have been intermittently (9) r______________ and have not (10) e______________!

Continuous reinforcement is best for (11) s______________ or teaching a new behavior, while it is best to switch to (12) i______________ reinforcement later for maintaining the behavior. With a continuous (13) s______________, extinction occurs rapidly, and with an intermittent schedule behavior is more durable, and (14) e______________ takes place gradually.

1. schedule	6. schedule	11. shaping
2. continually	7. maintaining	12. intermittent
3. schedule	8. intermittent	13. schedule
4. extinguish	9. reinforced	14. extinction
5. intermittently	10. extinguished	

EXAMPLE OF SCHEDULES OF REINFORCEMENT WITH CHILDREN

Author: Hopkins, B.L.

Title: Effects of candy and social reinforcement, instructions and reinforcement schedule leaning on the modification and maintenance of smiling.

Source: *Journal of Applied Behavior Analysis,* 1968, 1, 121-129.

Behavior: Smiling.

Scheduling: Candy given continuously and intermittently.

In this study Hopkins increased the frequency of smiling in two retarded boys by carefully adjusting the schedule of reinforcement and the kind of reinforcement. The boys showed very low rates of smiling. One boy was at first reinforced with candy every time he smiled during walks. He learned quickly with this continuous schedule. Candy reward was stopped and the behavior extinguished, or stopped, as well. Continuous reinforcement was started again, and the schedule was gradually leaned or thinned out to a much more intermittent schedule. Finally, social attention or social reinforcement was added (the child wore a sign saying, "If he smiles, talk to him. If he does not smile, ignore him."). And the sign too was eventually discontinued while the smiling continued. The (1) c______________ reinforcement (every time) was effective in starting the behavior, but extinction occurred rapidly. Later with an (2) i________________, or once-in-a-while schedule, and finally with (3) s________________ reinforcement, the smiling behavior was maintained.

---

1. continuous 2. intermittent 3. social

EXAMPLE OF SCHEDULES OF REINFORCEMENT WITH ADULTS

Authors: Kazdin, A.E., & Polster, R.

Title: Intermittent token reinforcement and response maintenance in extinction.

Source: *Behavior Therapy,* 1973, 4, 386-391.

Behavior: Verbal interactions.

Scheduling: Continuous and intermittent reinforcement.

This study took place in a sheltered workshop for mentally retarded adults. There was a comprehensive behavior modification program, a *token economy.* The two subjects were social isolates, and the program was designed to increase the frequency of social interactions. The patients were told they could earn tokens (exchangeable later) for talking with others during the three daily break periods. At first, both patients were reinforced every time, or continually, with tokens and the word "good."

During the second phase (praise but no token reinforcement), the behavior did extinguish, or stop, rapidly. Next, one patient was again reinforced on a continuous schedule, while the other was reinforced intermittently, or once in a while (first during two of the three breaks, and later during only one). Finally, with a return to praise but no token reinforcement, the social interactions of the patient on the continuous schedule again showed rapid extinction, but the person on the intermittent schedule showed longer lasting and stable behavior. That patient continued talking with others during breaks. Again, (1) c______________ reinforcement is very effective in learning behavior, but (2) i______________, or once-in-a-while reinforcement, results in behavior that does not stop or (3) e______________ as rapidly.

1. continuous 2. intermittent 3. extinguish

PRACTICE PAGE

This is the way that I might use the Principle of Schedules of Reinforcement:

1. BEHAVIOR TO BE CHANGED:

2. HOW THIS BEHAVIOR COULD BE MEASURED:

3. BEHAVIORAL PLAN (How I might use *schedules of reinforcement* in changing *this* behavior):

4. POSSIBLE ETHICAL AND LEGAL ISSUES:

Chapter 8

Principle of Social Reinforcement

IF A *SOCIAL* CONSEQUENCE (SUCH AS ATTENTION OR APPROVAL) HAS THE EFFECT OF *INCREASING* THE STRENGTH OR FREQUENCY OF THE BEHAVIOR THAT IT FOLLOWS, THEN *SOCIAL REINFORCEMENT* HAS TAKEN PLACE.

We are very social beings, and much of our behavior and learning is controlled by social (1) r______________. Our attention, approval, smiles, touching and nodding our heads yes are all kinds of (2) s______________ r______________. Much of our behavior and learning is not controlled directly by tangible rewards such as money or food, but rather by (3) s______________ r______________. As people mature from infancy to adulthood more and more of their behavior is controlled by (4) s______________ rewards. Paychecks are important, but so is the (5) a______________ and (6) a______________ of those we work with.

If we nod our heads yes and say, "Mm-hmm," every time a friend talks about a certain topic, chances are he will talk about that subject more because (7) n______________ our heads and saying (8) "M______________" are usually strong (9) s______________ r______________ for our friends. Also, we might shake our heads no, or withdraw our approval, and then we would be using social stimuli in a (10) p______________ way.

One beauty of (11) s______________ r______________ is that it is always available to us, we do not run out of it, it doesn't cost anything, and we can use it *immediately.* Remember that (12) i______________ reinforcement works best.

---

1. reinforcement
2. social reinforcement
3. social reinforcement
4. social
5. attention
6. approval
7. nodding
8. "mm-hmm"
9. social reinforcers
10. punishing
11. social reinforcement
12. immediate

EXAMPLE OF SOCIAL REINFORCEMENT WITH CHILDREN

Authors: Thomas, D.A., Nielson, L.J., Kuypers, D.S., & Becker, W.C.
Title: Social reinforcement and remedial instruction in the elimination of a classroom behavior problem.
Source: *The Journal of Special Education,* 1968, 2, 291-305.
Behavior: Disruptive classroom behavior.
Social Reinforcement: Teacher praise and attention.

While tangible reinforcers (stars, candy, etc.) and special activities (free time, recess, etc.) are available to teachers, the most readily available and often the most powerful reinforcers are social reinforcers such as teacher attention, approval, praise and physical contact. As we will see in Chapter 15, teachers may unwittingly be keeping undesirable classroom behavior going by paying attention to it. We may be giving attention to students who are being either disruptive or who are not doing their work. What Thomas et al. have done is demonstrate that a teacher's social approval can be used effectively to increase desirable classroom behavior. They set up experimental conditions of a low rate of approval, a high rate of approval, and finally, a high rate of social reinforcement combined with special tutoring. The low rate did produce some positive changes, the high rate showed still more improvement, but the combination demonstrated the greatest improvement of the three. Here, teacher attention or (1) s_________ r______________ was effective in increasing desirable classroom behavior. Since the attention given by the teacher increased the behavior that it was contingent upon, it is a form of (2) p____________ reinforcement.

---

1. social reinforcement 2. positive

It all started with a pat on the head
for bringing the paper in once last week!

EXAMPLE OF SOCIAL REINFORCEMENT WITH ADULTS

Author: Stumphauzer, J.S.
Title: Modification of delay choices in institutionalized youthful offenders through social reinforcement.
Source: *Psychonomic Science,* 1970, 18, 222-223.
Behavior: Delay of gratification.
Social Reinforcement: The words "good" or "mm-hmm."

To learn to delay immediate reward in favor of later, more valuable reward is an important part of the socialization process. Many delinquents and adult criminals do not delay gratification. In this study Stumphauzer was able to control the percentage of delay choices in four young adult prison inmates simply by showing approval (using the words "good" or "mm-hmm") after the desired response. There were a series of choices between something they could have immediately and something more valuable for which they would have to wait. They all started out by choosing immediate rewards almost every time, but the percentage of delay choices was then carefully controlled with contingent social approval. Here, (1) d______________ of gratification was controlled by contingent (2) s______________ approval or social (3) r______________.

1. delay 2. social 3. reinforcement

PRACTICE PAGE

This is the way I might use the Principle of Social Reinforcement:

1. BEHAVIOR TO BE CHANGED:

2. HOW THIS BEHAVIOR COULD BE MEASURED:

3. BEHAVIORAL PLAN (How I might use *social reinforcement* to change *this* behavior):

4. POSSIBLE ETHICAL AND LEGAL ISSUES:

Chapter 9

Principle of Generalization

BEHAVIOR THAT IS LEARNED UNDER CERTAIN CIRCUMSTANCES OR IN ONE SITUATION WILL OCCUR IN, OR *GENERALIZE* TO, OTHER SIMILAR SITUATIONS DEPENDING ON HOW SIMILAR THE SITUATIONS ARE.

We tend to do things we learn in one place, in other places as well, but this (1) g________________ depends, in part, on just how similar the two situations are. The more similar the two situations, the more likely (2) g________________ will occur. In order to insure that behavior will generalize from the place we are teaching it to another place, we should include in our learning situation as many of the stimuli from the generalization setting as possible. Generalization needs to be planned for or programmed!

If we want to teach a boy not to fight, we should work on this problem in a group situation with other boys who are (3) s________________ to the boys he fights with. If we worked on this alone with him we might try to teach him not to fight, but there is little chance that this would (4) g________________ to fighting opportunities later. Likewise, in teaching someone to be a printer, we would insure generalization if the training situation were as much (5) l________________ the work situation as possible, with respect to equipment, kinds of printing jobs, taking orders, etc.

Generalization is of key importance in education and behavior therapy. There is little (6) s________________ between living on a hospital ward and learning to adjust to community life, just as there is little similarity between learning to "be good" in prison and not committing crime later, on the streets. Education and therapy programs must maximize the chances for (7) g________________ by maximizing the (8) s________________ between the learning or treatment situation and the final generalization (9) s________________. This is why *community* intervention for problems in living and criminal behavior makes more sense than treatment in highly artificial mental hospitals and prisons, which would tend to (10) m________________ generalization.

1. generalization
2. generalization
3. similar
4. generalize
5. like
6. similarity
7. generalization
8. similarity
9. situation
10. minimize

EXAMPLE OF GENERALIZATION WITH CHILDREN

Authors: Blanchard, E.D., & Johnson, R.A.
Title: Generalization of operant classroom control procedures.
Source: *Behavior Therapy,* 1973, 4, 219-229.
Behaviors: Study, attention, inappropriate and disruptive behavior.
Generalization: From operant classroom to regular classroom.

There are many behavior modification programs in classrooms, and their effectiveness is well known. However, there is some question whether a behavioral or operant program during one class period will affect behavior during a second, regular class period. Does the behavior change generalize? Blanchard and Johnson measured the behavior of five seventh grade "behavior problem" students in two of their classes. Behaviors measured were appropriate study or attention, inappropriate but non-disruptive behavior, and disruptive classroom behavior.

In one class the experimenters used a systematically altered variety of consequences (ignoring, praising good behavior, scolding, and tangible rewards and punishments, e.g., privileges, soft drinks, etc.), while in a second class (regular classroom) they didn't use these contingencies. Tangible rewards were the most effective consequences both for getting behavior to change in the operant classroom and for getting the behavior to generalize to the other class period. Social reinforcements were less effective here: ignoring did not change behavior, while praise and scolding did affect behavior in the experimental class, although the change did not generalize to the second, non-experimental classroom setting. In this study, when (1) t________________ reinforcements and punishments were used in an experimental classroom, there was (2) g________________ to a separate, regular classroom.

---

1. tangible 2. generalization

EXAMPLE OF GENERALIZATION WITH ADULTS

Authors: Kale, R.I., Kaye, J., Whelan, P., & Hopkins, B.L.
Title: The effects of reinforcement on the modification, maintenance and generalization of social responses of mental patients.
Source: *Journal of Applied Behavior Analysis,* 1968, 1, 307-314.
Behavior: Social greeting responses.
Generalization: From the person doing the training to another person.

It is relatively easy to get behavior to change in a highly controlled situation, but more difficult to get the change to transfer or generalize to another setting, or to people other than the therapist. In this study, three adult, hospitalized male schizophrenics rarely greeted or interacted with staff or other patients. One experimenter then modified this behavior using prompts (say "Hi, Mr. __________!") and positive reinforcement (a cigarette and talk for 30 seconds). However, this behavior change did *not* transfer or generalize to a second staff member. Next, the patients were trained with five different experimenters, and then the behavior *did* generalize to the second staff person. It seems that experimental treatment or training with several staff (1) i______________ the probability that (2) g______________ to a variety of people will occur.

1. increases   2. generalization

PRACTICE PAGE

This is the way that I might use the Principle of Generalization:

1. BEHAVIOR TO BE CHANGED:

2. HOW THIS BEHAVIOR COULD BE MEASURED:

3. BEHAVIORAL PLAN (How I might get a change in *this* behavior to *generalize*):

4. POSSIBLE ETHICAL AND LEGAL ISSUES:

Chapter 10

Premack Principle

LOW PROBABILITY BEHAVIORS CAN BE *INCREASED* BY MAKING *HIGH PROBABILITY* BEHAVIORS CONTINGENT ON THEM.

The (1) P__________ Principle was named after psychologist David Premack, who first pointed to its application. We usually think of reinforcers as objects that we give someone. For example, M&M's can be reinforcing for children. However, the opportunity to engage in behaviors can be (2) r__________ too. High probability behaviors are those that are likely to occur (3) o__________ or a great deal of the time. If someone has free time, what is he most likely to do? Watch TV? Play sports? Read? Talk? Listen to music? If there is a high (4) p__________ that this person engages in a particular behavior, then we might assume that it is (5) r__________ for him to do so.

Low probability behaviors are those that are (6) n__________ often likely to occur. These may be the desired behaviors like homework, housework, etc. We can increase a low (7) p__________ behavior (homework) by making a (8) h__________ probability behavior (play outside) contingent upon it. This utilizes the (9) P__________ P__________, and with this contingency ("You can go out and play as soon as your homework is done.") we would expect doing homework to become (10) m__________ frequent. Contrast this with the less effective, "You can go out now if you will do your homework later!"

---

1. Premack
2. reinforcing
3. often
4. probability
5. reinforcing
6. not
7. probability
8. high
9. Premack Principle
10. more

EXAMPLE OF PREMACK PRINCIPLE WITH CHILDREN

Authors: Homme, L., deBaca, P., Devine, J., Steinhorst, R., & Rickert, E.

Title: Use of the Premack Principle in controlling the behavior of nursery school children.

Source: *Journal of the Experimental Analysis of Behavior,* 1963, 6, 544.

Behaviors: Sitting quietly, looking at the blackboard.

Reinforcement: Opportunity to run and scream.

These authors applied the Premack Principle quite literally in a nursery school classroom. Observing the children, they found a high incidence of running around the room, screaming, pushing chairs, etc. These were *high* probability behaviors, and therefore could be used to increase low probability behaviors in the classroom: sitting quietly in their chairs and looking at the blackboard. Intermittently, after they were sitting quietly and looking at the board, the teacher would ring a bell and tell the children to run and scream. Then she would sound another signal to stop them. Within a few days she had gained almost perfect control. Running and (1) s________________ (the high probability behaviors) were made contingent upon sitting quietly and (2) l________________ at the blackboard (the low probability behaviors). As suggested by the (3) P________________ P________________, sitting and looking then occurred more frequently.

1. screaming   2. looking   3. Premack Principle

EXAMPLE OF PREMACK PRINCIPLE WITH ADULTS

Authors: Gupton, T., & LeBow, M.D.
Title: Behavior management in a large industrial firm.
Source: *Behavior Therapy,* 1971, 2, 78-82.
Behavior: Selling service contracts.
Reinforcement: Selling renewal contracts.

The principles of behavior therapy are beginning to be applied in a wide variety of settings. Here, Gupton and LeBow, using the Premack Principle, have extended the application to an industrial firm. It seems that part-time telephone soliciters found it easy to sell renewal contracts. This was a high probability behavior to the extent that these sales were made to the exclusion of other kinds of sales. The opportunity to sell five renewal contracts was made contingent upon the sale of one service contract (a low probability behavior that the company wished to increase). Sales did increase significantly. Thus, even in so complex a situation as sales work, the (1) P______________ Principle was used to (2) i______________ low probability sales by making high probability sales (3) c______________ upon them.

1. Premack 2. increase 3. contingent

PRACTICE PAGE

This is the way that I might use the Premack Principle:

1. BEHAVIOR TO BE CHANGED:

2. HOW THIS BEHAVIOR COULD BE MEASURED:

3. BEHAVIORAL PLAN (How I might use the *Premack Principle* to change *this* behavior):

4. POSSIBLE ETHICAL AND LEGAL ISSUES:

Chapter 11

Principle of Assertion Training

UNASSERTIVE PEOPLE CAN BE TRAINED TO *ASSERT* THEMSELVES OR TO STAND UP FOR THEIR PERSONAL RIGHTS, AND THIS NEW ASSERTIVE BEHAVIOR WILL BE NATURALLY STRENGTHENED BY EITHER POSITIVE OR NEGATIVE REINFORCEMENT.

People who are shy, who "bottle up" feelings, or who allow themselves to be frequently taken advantage of can learn more adaptive behavior through (1) a______________ t______________.

Assertion training first educates individuals with regard to what their personal rights are, then utilizes a program based on several principles of behavior modification. Successive approximation or (2) s______________, behavior rehearsal, performance feedback, modeling and "homework" assignments are all important components of (3) a______________ t______________. Assertive behavior, by definition, causes either the termination of an aversive stimulus or the beginning of a positive one. Consequently, once an assertive response is made, you can expect the frequency of its occurrence to (4) i______________ because of the operation of either (5) p______________ or (6) n______________ reinforcement.

If a man has difficulty resisting unfair demands from his boss, (7) a______________ t______________ might prove helpful. We might begin by encouraging him to consider whether or not his personal (8) r______________ were being violated by his boss. We might (9) m______________ or role play a situation where the client acts in his own best interest and responds (10) a______________ without being overly aggressive or getting fired! We could also make use of assignments of progressively more difficult tasks or (11) "h______________" that he could try out during the week. Each completed assertive task would be likely to be reinforced either positively or negatively, and as a consequence would make assertive behavior more (12) p______________ in the future.

1. assertion training	5. positive	9. model
2. shaping	6. negative	10. assertively
3. assertion training	7. assertion training	11. "homework"
4. increase	8. rights	12. probable

EXAMPLE OF ASSERTION TRAINING WITH CHILDREN

Author: Gittelman, M.

Title: Behavior rehearsal as a technique in child treatment.

Source: *Journal of Child Psychology and Psychiatry,* 1965, 6, 251-255.

Behavior: Socially acceptable assertiveness.

Training: Rehearsal and reinforcement in a group.

Assertiveness and aggressiveness are sometimes confused. Assertion training does not necessarily mean that we are training people to fight or to be more aggressive. Rather, we are training them to emit more *socially acceptable* assertiveness. In this study, Gittelman worked with a group of boys who, when provoked, would very often fight or attack. They were too aggressive, or more accurately, their assertiveness was not socially acceptable and was not really adaptive for them.

In group therapy meetings they would explore what kind of situation would provoke each boy, and then practice the situations in the group. The boys would get negative points for fighting or "blowing-up," and positive points for handling the provocation in an assertive, yet socially adaptive manner. One point was given for reacting in a more passive manner, while two points were given for a response which disarmed or reduced the threat of the instigator. In the one case discussed in detail, the boy learned to handle these situations in the group within four sessions. Furthermore, the behavior generalized to outside the group. With timid children, or children like these who are aggressive, and yet are not appropriately assertive, (1) a____________ training can help them stand up for their rights in socially adaptive or (2) a____________ ways.

---

1. assertion 2. appropriate

I'm not gonna tell him to put his wings down. **You** want him to put his wings down, **you** tell him to put his wings down.

EXAMPLE OF ASSERTION TRAINING WITH ADULTS

Author: Bloomfield, H.H.

Title: Assertive training in an outpatient group of chronic schizophrenics: A preliminary report.

Source: *Behavior Therapy,* 1973, 4, 277-281.

Behavior: Assertiveness.

Training: Role playing in a group, rehearsal and practice.

Chronic schizophrenics tend to be shy, compliant and submissive. This may especially be a problem when they are outpatients because they often withdraw, keep to themselves, and do not appropriately stand up for their legitimate rights. In this paper, Bloomfield reports working with a group of 8 to 10 previously hospitalized patients of this type. One patient, a 33-year-old woman, was very compliant and was being intimidated by a neighbor. Her problem was discussed and further analyzed in the group. Other group members were encouraged to model their assertiveness. Role rehearsal, with someone playing the neighbor, was implemented, and then roles were reversed so that others could model appropriate assertiveness. She was taught and practiced expressing displeasure, and also to present it in a way that would facilitate more pleasant interactions. This new assertiveness was tried successfully with the neighbor, which led to a mutual understanding and an improved relationship. Thus, the newly acquired (1) a_______________ met with (2) p_______________ r_______________, and we would expect it to become more frequent.

---

1. assertiveness 2. positive reinforcement

PRACTICE PAGE

This is the way I might use the Principle of Assertion Training:

1. BEHAVIOR TO BE CHANGED:

2. HOW THIS BEHAVIOR COULD BE MEASURED:

3. BEHAVIORAL PLAN (How I might use *assertion training* to change *this* behavior):

4. POSSIBLE ETHICAL AND LEGAL ISSUES:

O.K., I can take a hint, I'll turn it down from now on.

Principles for Decreasing Behavior

Chapter 12

Principle of Punishment 1 Aversive Stimulation

IF THE *PRESENTATION* OF AN *AVERSIVE* STIMULUS AS THE CONSEQUENCE OF A BEHAVIOR *DECREASES* THE STRENGTH OR FREQUENCY OF THAT BEHAVIOR, THEN PUNISHMENT 1, *AVERSIVE STIMULATION*, HAS TAKEN PLACE.

As we have seen, *both* positive reinforcement *and* negative reinforcement act to (1) i______________ the behavior they follow. Punishment is quite different, it *decreases* or *suppresses* the behavior it follows. (2) P______________ decreases the strength or frequency of behavior, at least temporarily. Punishment (3) d______________ behavior.

There are three kinds of punishment that (4) d______________ behavior. In Punishment 1, aversive or painful stimulation is used to stop a behavior. A behavior occurs and is followed by (5) a______________ or painful consequences which have the effect of decreasing that behavior, at least for a while. Each time a child reaches for an expensive lamp we slap his hand. The behavior is (6) r______________ for the lamp and the (7) s______________ on the hand is the aversive consequence. We expect the frequency of this behavior to (8) d______________ because of (9) P______________ 1 which uses (10) a______________ or unpleasant consequences to decrease or stop behavior.

While Punishment 1 and negative reinforcement both make use of aversive stimulation, and are often confused, they are *very* different. Punishment follows behavior and acts to *decrease* or *suppress* it. With negative reinforcement, however, the behavior terminates or "turns off" existing aversive stimuli which results in that behavior occurring *more* often. In one, the behavior is (11) p______________, in the other it is (12) r______________ with the stopping of pain.

1. increase
2. punishment
3. decreases
4. decrease
5. aversive
6. reaching
7. slap
8. decrease
9. punishment
10. aversive
11. punished
12. reinforced

EXAMPLE OF PUNISHMENT 1: AVERSIVE STIMULATION WITH CHILDREN

Authors: O'Leary, K.D., Kaufman, K.F., Kass, R.E., & Drabman, R.S.
Title: The effects of loud and soft reprimands on the behavior of disruptive students.
Source: *Exceptional Children,* 1970, 37, 145-155.
Behavior: Disruptive classroom behavior.
Punishment: Loud and soft reprimands.

Verbal reprimands in the classroom ("Stop it!" "Sit down!" "No!" etc.) are usually considered a form of punishment. What O'Leary et al. have found, however, is that loud reprimands (audible to the whole class) may in fact positively reinforce, maintain, or even increase undesirable behavior. These may focus attention on the disruptive student and set up opportunities for attention from peers. In this study they compared the effects of loud (audible to class) and soft (audible only to the one child) reprimands. They found, in fact, that disruptive behavior decreased most under the condition of soft reprimand. Loud reprimands in the classroom may actually act to (1) r__________ disruptive behavior, while O'Leary et al. show that soft reprimands do act to (2) p__________ or decrease the frequency of the behavior they follow.

1. reinforce 2. punish

EXAMPLE OF PUNISHMENT 1: AVERSIVE STIMULATION WITH ADULTS

Author: Kohlenberg, R.J.
Title: The punishment of persistent vomiting: A case study.
Source: *Journal of Applied Behavior Analysis,* 1970, 3, 241-245.
Behavior: Vomiting.
Punishment: Contingent electric shock.

Persistent vomiting is a great danger because of the resultant weight loss. In this case reported by Kohlenberg, a 21-year-old, hospitalized, retarded woman was reported to vomit after every meal. She had been steadily losing weight over the previous three months. At the beginning of the study she weighed 74 pounds. The series of behaviors related to vomiting were studied and it was decided to punish an early behavior in the chain: observable abdominal stomach tension.

After each meal, the patient was seated in an experimental room, closely observed, and shocked with an electric prod whenever the stomach tension was observed. At first, this resulted in a transitory increase in the behavior (as is fairly common with punishment), and then a gradual decrease of stomach tensions and vomiting. There was a gradual weight gain and the health hazard was eliminated. (Once again, the use of painful stimuli in treatments such as this requires careful consideration of ethical and legal issues.) Here life-threatening vomiting behavior was stopped by the contingent (1) p__________ of observable stomach (2) t__________, an early link in the series of behaviors leading to vomiting.

1. punishment 2. tension

PRACTICE PAGE

This is the way that I might use the Principle of Punishment 1, Aversive Stimulation:

1. BEHAVIOR TO BE CHANGED:

2. HOW THIS BEHAVIOR COULD BE MEASURED:

3. BEHAVIORAL PLAN (How I might use *Punishment 1, aversive stimulation*, to change *this* behavior):

4. POSSIBLE ETHICAL AND LEGAL ISSUES:

Chapter 13

Principle of Punishment 2 Time-Out

IF THE *OPPORTUNITY* FOR *POSITIVE REINFORCEMENT* IS *WITHDRAWN* FOR A BRIEF PERIOD AS THE CONSEQUENCE OF A BEHAVIOR, AND THE EFFECT IS A *DECREASE* IN THE STRENGTH OR FREQUENCY OF THAT BEHAVIOR, THEN PUNISHMENT 2, *TIME-OUT FROM POSITIVE REINFORCEMENT,* HAS TAKEN PLACE.

Reinforcement, regardless of whether it is positive or negative, has the effect of (1) i______________ the behavior it follows. Punishment, *regardless* of type, has the effect of (2) d______________ the behavior it follows. Both aversive stimulation and time-out (3) d______________ behavior. With (4) t__________-o__________ we try to decrease a behavior not by adding an aversive or painful stimulus as in Punishment 1, but rather by *withdrawing* or *removing* the opportunity for positive reinforcement in Punishment 2. This is called time-out from (5) p______________ r______________ and has the effect of (6) d______________ the particular behavior it follows.

If attention we give someone acts as a positive reinforcer, then taking away the opportunity to get our attention or ignoring him may act as (7) P______________ 2 or (8) t__________-o__________. If we can stop a patient in a psychiatric hospital from going on tangents in his conversation by turning away for a minute, ignoring or taking away our attention each time he does it, then we have used time-out or punishment type (9) t__________. The behavior is "going off on (10) t______________," and the punishment is removal of the (11) o______________ for getting attention.

If we use aversive stimulation to stop a behavior it is (12) P______________ 1. If we remove the opportunity for positive reinforcement to stop a behavior it is Punishment 2, or (13) t__________-o__________.

---

1. increasing
2. decreasing
3. decrease
4. time-out
5. positive reinforcement
6. decreasing
7. punishment
8. time-out
9. two
10. tangents
11. opportunity
12. punishment
13. time-out

EXAMPLE OF PUNISHMENT 2: TIME-OUT WITH CHILDREN

Authors: Bishop, B.R., & Stumphauzer, J.S.
Title: Behavior therapy of thumbsucking in children: A punishment (time-out) and generalization effect – what's a mother to do?
Source: *Psychological Reports,* 1973, 33, 939-944.
Behavior: Thumbsucking.
Time-Out: Temporary loss of opportunity to watch TV cartoons.

It is apparent from the avid attention that children give Saturday morning cartoons, that watching them is a reinforcing activity. In this study, Bishop and Stumphauzer were able to stop thumbsucking in three young children by using the principle of time-out. A remote on/off switch was connected to a small television set. These children were observed while watching Saturday morning cartoons and it was found that they indeed sucked their thumbs at a high rate (baseline). During four treatment sessions the cartoons were turned off whenever the child placed his thumb in his mouth (time-out from positive reinforcement). And the TV was turned on again when thumbsucking ceased (positive reinforcement). This temporary loss of opportunity to watch TV cartoons or (1) t__________-o__________ from reinforcement had the effect of greatly reducing the amount of thumbsucking both in the treatment office and during storytime in the nursery school (generalization). Time-out from TV cartoons had the effect of reducing or (2) d________________ the frequency of thumbsucking.

---

1. time-out 2. decreasing

EXAMPLE OF PUNISHMENT 2: TIME-OUT WITH ADULTS

Authors: Adams, M.R., & Popelka, G.
Title: The influence of "time-out" on stutterers and their dysfluency.
Source: *Behavior Therapy,* 1971, 2, 234-239.
Behavior: Stuttering.
Time-Out: 10 seconds of no talking.

It has been suggested that speech is a self-reinforcing behavior. If this is true, then time-out, or a temporary withdrawal of the opportunity to speak, would constitute a punishment. This kind of time-out was applied by Adams and Popelka to eight young adult stutterers. In the treatment condition, when they would stutter while reading a series of passages, they would have to stop for 10 seconds (time-out). There was no such time-out during comparison control sessions. In both kinds of sessions they decreased their stuttering (as is usually true when re-reading material); but, the time-out treatment did decrease stuttering more quickly. In this case (1) t__________-o__________ from speaking was effective in decreasing (2) s________________. This suggests that time-out from speaking does function as (3) p________________.

---

1. time-out 2. stuttering 3. punishment

PRACTICE PAGE

This is the way that I might use the Principle of Punishment 2, Time-Out:

1. BEHAVIOR TO BE CHANGED:

2. HOW THIS BEHAVIOR COULD BE MEASURED:

3. BEHAVIORAL PLAN (How I might use *Punishment 2, time-out*, to change *this* behavior):

4. POSSIBLE ETHICAL AND LEGAL ISSUES:

Chapter 14

Principle of Punishment 3 Response Cost

IF *POSITIVE REINFORCEMENT* IS *LOST OR TAKEN AWAY* AS THE CONSEQUENCE OF A BEHAVIOR, AND THE EFFECT IS A *DECREASE* IN THE STRENGTH OR FREQUENCY OF THAT BEHAVIOR, THEN PUNISHMENT 3, *RESPONSE COST*, HAS TAKEN PLACE.

A third type of punishment is response cost in which the behavior or response actually (1) c__________ something. A positive reinforcer is taken away as the consequence of a behavior. Like the other two kinds of punishment, response cost has the effect of (2) d__________ or suppressing the behavior it follows. One everyday example of response cost is a traffic ticket. The behavior or response may have been speeding and the (3) r__________ c__________, the ticket and loss of money or driver's license.

In a token economy (see Chapter 21), the unwanted or undesirable behavior may result in a contingent loss of (4) t__________. Similarly, if a student is earning points in a classroom for academic and productive social behavior and he gets into a fight, that fighting behavior may (5) c__________ him a set number of (6) p__________.

All three kinds of punishment act to decrease or at least temporarily (7) s__________ the behavior they follow. In Punishment 1, aversive stimulation, the behavior results in (8) a__________ or even painful consequences. In Punishment 2, time-out, the behavior results in a time-out or temporary loss of opportunity to earn (9) p__________ r__________. Finally, in Punishment 3, response cost, the behavior actually (10) c__________ something — there is a set fine or loss of reinforcement.

---

1. costs
2. decreasing
3. response cost
4. tokens
5. cost
6. points
7. suppress
8. aversive
9. positive reinforcers
10. costs

EXAMPLE OF PUNISHMENT 3: RESPONSE COST WITH CHILDREN

Authors: Kaufman, K.F., & O'Leary, K.D.
Title: Reward, cost, and self-evaluation procedures for disruptive adolescents in a psychiatric hospital school.
Source: *Journal of Applied Behavior Analysis,* 1972, 5, 293-309.
Behavior: Variety of behavior in classrooms.
Response Cost: Loss of tokens.

This study is of special interest here because it compares the effectiveness of two principles of behavior modification in two experimental classrooms for hospitalized adolescents. In one classroom, students were reinforced with tokens for productive classroom behavior. In the other classroom, students were given 10 tokens at the beginning of each period which they could keep. However, in this second classroom misbehavior would *cost* the students a set number of tokens. Using a baseline design, both systems were stopped for a while (to see if behavior would return to the pre-token level) and then the two programs were switched in the two classrooms to insure that if there was a difference it would not just be due to a difference in classrooms or students.

In this comparative study *both* programs worked about equally well – both were more effective in reducing disruptive and deviant behavior than before they were started (baseline condition). However, no attempt was made to compare the possible long-range effects of using this form of punishment rather than reinforcement. In this study the students in one classroom earned tokens, (1) p________________ r________________, and in the other they had tokens and lost them for disruptive and deviant behavior, (2) r______________ c__________.

Both positive reinforcement and punishment were effective in changing or (3) m________________ behavior in these classrooms.

---

1. positive reinforcers 2. response cost 3. modifying

EXAMPLE OF PUNISHMENT 3: RESPONSE COST WITH ADULTS

Authors: Harmatz, M.G., & Lapuc, P.
Title: Behavior modification of overeating in a psychiatric population.
Source: *Journal of Consulting and Clinical Psychology,* 1968, 32, 583-587.
Behavior: Overeating.
Response Cost: Loss of money for failure to lose weight.

This is a study of obese patients in a Veterans Administration psychiatric hospital. All patients were routinely given a money allotment of five dollars for personal use (typically used for cigarettes, snacks, etc.). In this study there was a comparison of three different treatment strategies. The 21 overweight patients in this study were all placed on an 1800 calorie a day diet for regular meals, but were not restricted in their snacking.

One group received only the diet everyone was on and they received the five dollar allotment regardless of weight. A second group received weekly group therapy centered on exploring "underlying causes" of overeating; they also received the five dollar allotment noncontingently. In the third, the behavior modification group, patients *lost* a proportion of their money allotment if they did not lose weight each week. Both response cost and group therapy resulted in more weight loss than the diet-only group, but response cost was most effective in weight loss during treatment *and* at follow-up. In this example of response cost the response was (1) g________________ weight and the (2) c________________ was loss of (3) m________________.

1. gaining 2. cost 3. money

PRACTICE PAGE

This is the way that I might use the Principle of Punishment 3. Response Cost:

1. BEHAVIOR TO BE CHANGED:

2. HOW THIS BEHAVIOR COULD BE MEASURED:

3. BEHAVIORAL PLAN (How I might use *Punishment 3, response cost*, to change *this* behavior):

4. POSSIBLE ETHICAL AND LEGAL ISSUES:

Chapter 15

Principle of Extinction

WHEN BEHAVIOR IS NO LONGER FOLLOWED BY REINFORCEMENT, THE BEHAVIOR WILL *DECREASE* IN STRENGTH OR FREQUENCY AND WILL GRADUALLY *EXTINGUISH.*

Reinforcement, regardless of whether it is positive or negative, has the effect of (1) i________________ the behavior it follows. Punishment, regardless of type, has the effect of (2) d________________ the behavior it follows. Aversive stimulation, time-out, and response cost (3) d________________ behavior, at least temporarily.

Extinction is another procedure for decreasing behavior, and it has more lasting effects. If we simply *stop* the reinforcement that initially increased a behavior, the behavior will decrease in frequency and we call this effect (4) e________________. If we pick up a baby each time he cries, he may be learning to cry because our attention may serve as a (5) p________________ r________________ and act to increase the number of times he cries. We might get him to cry less or unlearn the crying by spanking him each time he cried, in this case using (6) p________________, or more exactly (7) a________________ s________________. But it might be better to simply stop reinforcing the behavior, to use (8) e________________. If we stopped giving our attention or stopped (9) r________________ crying, then we should expect the behavior to gradually (10) d________________ or extinguish.

How quickly extinction occurs depends, in part, on the schedule of reinforcement used when the behavior was being learned. If a continuous, or every-time (11) s________________ of reinforcement is used, extinction will occur rapidly. However, if an intermittent, or once-in-a-while schedule is used, (12) e________________ takes longer. Therefore, if we do not want a behavior to extinguish easily we would select an (13) i________________ schedule of reinforcement.

1. increasing	6. punishment	11. schedule
2. decreasing	7. aversive stimulation	12. extinction
3. decrease	8. extinction	13. intermittent
4. extinction	9. reinforcing	
5. positive reinforcer	10. decrease	

EXAMPLE OF EXTINCTION WITH CHILDREN

Authors: Zimmerman, E.H., & Zimmerman, J.

Title: The alteration of behavior in a special classroom situation.

Source: *Journal of the Experimental Analysis of Behavior,* 1962, 5, 59-60.

Behavior: Unproductive classroom behavior.

Extinction: Removal of attention.

Inadvertently, we often reinforce undesirable behavior by paying attention to it. This is often especially true in the classroom when the teacher or aide gives more attention to either the student who is *not* doing well, or focuses on disruptive students. The wheel that squeaks the loudest gets the most grease. Such attention can be viewed as social reinforcement, and may be *maintaining* the behaviors we are concerned about. This is precisely what Zimmerman and Zimmerman found with two 11-year-old students.

One boy did not spell well, and the teacher would spend a lot of time with him when he missed a word. His spelling did not improve, but rather he took more and more of her time. Then she started to use extinction by not paying attention to him when he misspelled a word. At the same time she showed approval when he was correct. Within a month his spelling was consistently better and other undesirable behaviors dropped out as well.

O.K. Snookums, I promise, no more canned food;
only please take me off extinction!

A second 11-year-old was more disruptive and often displayed temper tantrums which invariably resulted in the formation of a group of staff around him. Again, it appeared that the attention may have been maintaining the undesirable behavior. Using the principle of extinction, the teacher isolated the boy when he began a tantrum, ignored him, and later gave him attention when he displayed productive behavior. Tantrum behavior extinguished. In both cases teacher attention seemed to (1) r____________ the unproductive classroom behavior. By removing attention that had maintained the behavior, these behaviors gradually stopped or (2) e____________.

1. reinforce 2. extinguished

EXAMPLE OF EXTINCTION WITH ADULTS

Author: Agras, W.S.
Title: Behavior therapy in the management of chronic schizophrenia.
Source: *American Journal of Psychiatry,* 1967, 124, 240-243.
Behavior: Refusing to eat.
Extinction: Stopped paying attention to not eating.

In this paper Agras reports treatment of a 34-year-old man who had been treated in institutions since adolescence. One constant problem was his refusal to eat, and he weighed only 87 pounds. He often did not eat even though nursing staff would spend a great deal of time constantly urging him to do so. It was thought that the attention may have been reinforcing and was maintaining the behavior of not eating. All such reinforcement was removed by making food available to him at certain times and not giving attention when he refused to eat. Eating did increase to a satisfactory level during the next five days. He was discharged to a rehabilitation setting where a similar program was followed, and he reached a weight of 104 pounds. In this case, the nursing staff seem to have been inadvertently (1) r______________ not eating by urging and coaxing. When this reinforcement was stopped (2) e______________ of "not eating" occurred.

---

1. reinforcing 2. extinction

PRACTICE PAGE

This is the way that I might use the Principle of Extinction:

1. BEHAVIOR TO BE CHANGED:

2. HOW THIS BEHAVIOR COULD BE MEASURED:

3. BEHAVIORAL PLAN (How I might arrange for *this* behavior to *extinguish*):

4. POSSIBLE ETHICAL AND LEGAL ISSUES:

Chapter 16

Principle of Counterconditioning

IN COUNTERCONDITIONING, AN UNWANTED OR UNADAPTIVE BEHAVIOR IS ELIMINATED BY CONDITIONING A NEW, *INCOMPATIBLE* BEHAVIOR IN ITS PLACE.

Some behaviors are incompatible; they don't go together. You can not be afraid and relaxed at the same time. Fear and relaxation are (1) i________________ behaviors.

Fears, phobias and anxieties can be eliminated by applying the principle of (2) c________________. First, you must determine what the particular stimuli that lead to the fear are. In a fear of high places, the behavior is (3) f________________, and the stimulus that leads to fear is (4) h________________ places. The fear might be eliminated if we can find a behavior that doesn't go together with fear, or is (5) i________________ with fear. One such behavior is relaxation. Relaxation and fear are (6) i________________.

A *hierarchy* (or list) of feared situations is established from least feared to most feared. In this example, a first item in the (7) h________________ might be standing on a short ladder. A high item on the hierarchy would be looking down from a second story window. We would then teach the person how to completely relax, and then *while he is relaxed*, to have him *gradually* imagine that he is in higher and higher places. With many trys we can then link or condition the stimuli of (8) h________________ places with the new response of (9) r________________, and this process is called (10) c________________.

---

1. incompatible
2. counterconditioning
3. fear
4. high
5. incompatible
6. incompatible
7. hierarchy
8. high
9. relaxation
10. counterconditioning

EXAMPLE OF COUNTERCONDITIONING WITH CHILDREN

Authors: Lazarus, A.A., & Abramovitz, A.

Title: The use of "emotive imagery" in the treatment of children's phobias.

Source: *Journal of Mental Science,* 1962, 108, 191-195.

Behaviors: Children's phobias and fears.

Counterconditioning: Development of incompatible, pleasurable feelings in the child's imagination.

It is difficult to train children to simply relax in the presence of fear-making stimuli. Instead, Lazarus and Abramovitz have developed the technique of emotive imagery. In initial interviews they determine the particular circumstances, and write out a hierarchy (list), or ranking of fears from least feared to most feared object or situation. Next, they note the child's hero images (those on television, in movies, or imagination that are particularly powerful and important to him). As the therapy starts, the child is asked to imagine everyday scenes with his hero present. Then gradually, when it is judged that the child can well imagine the hero in his life, the lowest fear-making stimulus is introduced, and the child and hero handle it.

With this accomplished (fear extinguished), they proceed up the hierarchy. The strong positive feelings and trust for the hero are incompatible with fear. In this particular study, three cases were presented: fear of dogs, fear of the dark and fear of school. All of the children improved greatly in a few sessions. Here, the counterconditioning, or, more specifically, (1) e__________ i__________ was applied successfully by pairing strong positive feelings for (2) h__________ with fear-making stimuli.

1. emotive imagery 2. heroes

See Jimmy, there's absolutely no reason to be afraid of the nice doggy.

EXAMPLE OF COUNTERCONDITIONING WITH ADULTS

Author: Wolpe, J.

Title: The systematic desensitization treatment of neuroses.

Source: *The Journal of Nervous and Mental Disease,* 1961, 132, 189-203.

Behaviors: Anxiety, phobias, etc.

Counterconditioning: Gradual substitution of relaxation for anxiety.

Joseph Wolpe has developed a widely used technique which he terms "systematic desensitization." In this paper, he presents his technique and its results with 39 patients. The method first involves careful history taking, especially relating to problem areas. Next, the patient is taught deep muscle relaxation (since it is incompatible with anxiety and will be used to replace it later). Then a hierarchy of anxiety-producing situations is constructed by listing them in order from least to most anxiety provoking. Finally, in the systematic desensitization procedure itself, these stimuli are presented in the patient's imagination while he is relaxed, beginning with the least anxiety-making stimulus. Because of the relaxed state, the anxiety decreases and the patient gradually moves up the hierarchy an item at a time until it is completed. The stimuli that once led to anxiety are now associated with relaxation. Wolpe reports good results with most patients. In this form of counterconditioning called (1) s____________ desensitization, neurotic (2) a____________ is gradually replaced with an incompatible behavior like (3) r____________.

1. systematic 2. anxiety 3. relaxation

PRACTICE PAGE

This is the way that I might use the Principle of Counterconditioning:

1. BEHAVIOR TO BE CHANGED:

2. HOW THIS BEHAVIOR COULD BE MEASURED:

3. BEHAVIORAL PLAN (How I might use *counterconditioning* to change *this* behavior):

4. POSSIBLE ETHICAL AND LEGAL ISSUES:

Chapter 17

Principle of Negative Practice

PRACTICING A BAD HABIT OVER AND OVER AGAIN, ON A REQUIRED SCHEDULE, LEADS TO EXTINCTION OF THAT BEHAVIOR BECAUSE OF INHIBITION AND THE ABSENCE OF REINFORCEMENT.

Many bad habits such as nail biting, stuttering and tics have been eliminated by (1) n______________ practice. The habit must be practiced over and over and (2) o______________ again. Theoretically, an inhibition to performing that behavior builds up with (3) n______________ p______________.

If a child is a problem nail biter, we might have him (4) b__________ his fingernails for several minutes every hour on the hour. Gradually, we would expect an (5) i______________ for nail biting to build up, and for him to decrease or (6) s______________ biting his nails as he was before. This would be due to (7) n______________ p______________.

Performing the behavior during negative practice might become uncomfortable, fatiguing, painful or punishing. So, in addition to inhibiting nail biting, *not* nail biting or *stopping* nail biting would be a relief or would be rewarding or (8) r______________.

1. negative
2. over
3. negative practice
4. bite
5. inhibition
6. stop
7. negative practice
8. reinforcing

EXAMPLE OF NEGATIVE PRACTICE WITH CHILDREN

Author: Walton, D.

Title: Experimental psychology and the treatment of a ticqueur.

Source: *Journal of Child Psychology and Psychiatry,* 1961, 2, 148-155.

Behavior: Tics.

Negative Practice: Massed repetition of the tics.

This study deals with the treatment of an 11-year-old boy who had exhibited mild facial tics (slight, involuntary movements of the mouth and face) for six years. During the year before treatment he developed other major tics: sudden jerking of arms and legs with explosive utterances such as, "good, good, good." Once a day for 20 days he was instructed and supervised in doing the major tic behavior (jerking and saying "good") repetitively for about 30 minutes. He then practiced the remaining tics for a total of 36 sessions. Tics were reduced to zero frequency with the exception of an infrequent mild facial tic, and this progress was still holding at a one-year follow-up. In this case mild and severe (1) t_______________ were eliminated by massed practice of the tic, or by (2) n_______________ p_______________.

1. tics   2. negative practice

EXAMPLE OF NEGATIVE PRACTICE WITH ADULTS

Author: Keutzer, C.S.

Title: Behavior modification of smoking: The experimental investigation of diverse techniques.

Source: *Behaviour Research and Therapy,* 1968, 6, 137-157.

Behavior: Smoking.

Negative Practice: Massed practice of smoking.

Controlling smoking behavior is receiving a great deal of attention, and negative practice is one promising method for stopping the habit. Keutzer compared a number of techniques: (1) "covarant control therapy" in which people are taught to manage their own contingencies; (2) aversive conditioning utilizing breath holding; (3) a placebo

You're really serious about using negative practice
to cut down on cigarette smoking, aren't you Harry!

drug therapy; and, (4) negative practice. The negative practice group smoked several cigarettes in quick succession in a small smoke-filled room during treatment sessions, and if they yielded to their desire to smoke at home they were to carry out practice sessions there as well. Fifty-eight percent of those treated with negative practice greatly reduced their smoking by the end of the study and 33 stopped completely. Here, (1) n______________ p______________ is repetitive smoking, with many members of the group showing a resultant (2) d______________ in smoking behavior.

---

1. negative practice 2. decrease

PRACTICE PAGE

This is the way that I might use the Principle of Negative Practice:

1. BEHAVIOR TO BE CHANGED:

2. HOW THIS BEHAVIOR COULD BE MEASURED:

3. BEHAVIORAL PLAN (How I might use *negative practice* to change *this* behavior):

4. POSSIBLE ETHICAL AND LEGAL ISSUES:

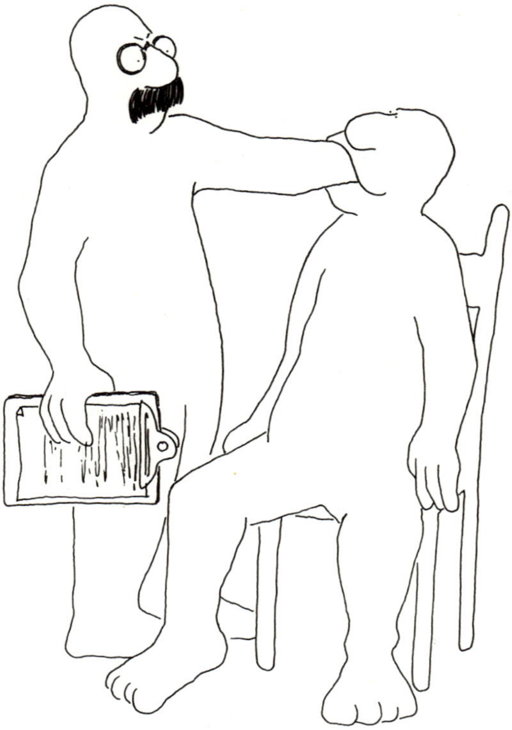

Your fingernails, Mr. Sprague, not mine!

Additional Principles

Chapter 18

Principle of Deprivation and Satiation

THE REINFORCING CHARACTERISTICS OF A STIMULUS MAY BE *INCREASED* IF THE PERSON IS DEPRIVED OF THAT STIMULUS, OR MAY BE *DECREASED* BY MAKING IT ABUNDANT TO THE POINT OF SATIATION.

One thing that determines the effectiveness of a reinforcer is how much it is available to the person; in short, whether he's had too little of it or too much of it.

If a person is deprived of a stimulus that is usually rewarding to him, the reinforcer will become even *more* effective. Deprivation (1) i_______________ the reinforcing power of a stimulus. If a child likes ice cream and hasn't had any in a long time, or has been (2) d_______________ of ice cream, then ice cream will be a strong (3) r_______________ for him.

The opposite is true with satiation. If a person has *too much* of a rewarding thing, it will lose its reinforcing properties. He will become sated or (4) s_______________ will occur with regard to that particular reinforcer. Satiation (5) d_______________ the reinforcing power of a stimulus. If the same child is given three large ice cream sundaes to eat and then is offered an ice cream cone as a reward for doing something, chances are this will not be much of an incentive for him. At that moment (6) s_______________ will probably have taken place and he won't want any more ice cream.

By altering how available a given reinforcing stimulus is, we can change its reinforcing power. (7) D_______________ *in*creases reinforcing power while (8) s_______________ *de*creases the power of a reinforcer.

1. increases	5. decreases
2. deprived	6. satiation
3. reinforcer or reward	7. deprivation
4. satiation	8. satiation

EXAMPLE OF DEPRIVATION AND SATIATION WITH CHILDREN

Authors: Lovaas, O.I., Freitag, G., Kindler, M.I., Rubenstein, B.D., Schaeffer, B., & Simmons, J.Q.

Title: Establishment of social reinforcers in schizophrenic children using food.

Source: *Journal of Experimental Child Psychology,* 1966, 4, 109-125.

Behaviors: Responding to commands, bar pressing.

Deprivation: Withholding of meals / food reinforcement given during sessions.

This group of investigators report work with twin schizophrenic children. They developed social reinforcers in these children who did not respond to words like "good." By repeatedly pairing food and "good," the word "good" alone soon began to function as a positive reinforcer. To assure that the food reinforcers would have their maximum effect, the children were not given food in regular meals (deprivation), but rather, they received the food as reinforcement in training sessions. Effective social reinforcers were developed with this procedure. (The moral issue of depriving children of food should be considered when dealing with a procedure such as this.) In this case, the (1) d____________ of food probably did increase the (2) r____________ properties of the food in training sessions. If the children had been fed just before sessions, we would expect that food in sessions would have less reinforcing power. (3) S____________ might have taken place.

1. deprivation 2. reinforcing 3. satiation

EXAMPLE OF DEPRIVATION AND SATIATION WITH ADULTS

Author: Ayllon, T.
Title: Intensive treatment of psychotic behavior by stimulus satiation and food reinforcement.
Source: *Behaviour Research and Therapy,* 1963, 1, 53-61.
Behavior: Hoarding towels in a hospital.
Satiation: Making towels plentiful.

This classic study by Ayllon reports a segment of the treatment of a 47-year-old patient diagnosed as chronic schizophrenic. One of her behaviors was hoarding hospital towels in her room. Even though they were removed from her room twice a week, she still managed to hoard between 19 and 29 at all times (baseline). Rather than take them away, Ayllon decided to use satiation. Nurses were to stop by her room to give her towels without comment: seven towels daily for the first week, up to 60 a day for the third week! When the towels in her room reached about 600 (dresser, bed, all of the furniture and floor were covered with towels), the patient started taking a few of them out. The staff didn't give her any more towels, and the number found in her room gradually dropped to from one to five. At first she said things like, "Thank you," but finally said, "Get these dirty towels out of here." We can assume that initially the towels had (1) r_______________ properties, but when they were too plentiful the reinforcing properties decreased or (2) s_______________ took place.

1. reinforcing 2. satiation

PRACTICE PAGE

This is the way that I might use the Principle of Deprivation and Satiation:

1. BEHAVIOR TO BE CHANGED:

2. HOW THIS BEHAVIOR COULD BE MEASURED:

3. BEHAVIORAL PLAN (How I might use *deprivation* or *satiation* in changing *this* behavior):

4. POSSIBLE ETHICAL AND LEGAL ISSUES:

Chapter 19

Principle of Modeling and Imitation

BEHAVIOR MAY BE LEARNED OR MODIFIED SIMPLY AS A FUNCTION OF *OBSERVING* THE BEHAVIOR OF A MODEL, AND BY *OBSERVING* THE CONSEQUENCES OF THE MODEL'S BEHAVIOR.

Much of what we learn is by watching or observing someone else do it first, and then trying it ourselves. This learning process is called modeling or imitation. The person who displays the behavior may be called a (1) m________________.

Most of our complicated behavior and skills are learned by (2) m________________ and (3) i________________. In learning to be afraid or not afraid, a child closely watches his parents' and friends' behavior. They are his (4) m________________. If we are learning a new, complicated skill like driving a car, it would take forever if there were simply rewards, punishments and gradual shaping. Instead, we carefully watch someone else drive and then (5) i________________ him.

Whether models are imitated or not depends on several factors. If they are attractive, important, and rewarded for what they do, then it is more likely that they will be effective (6) m________________ and will be (7) i________________. Conversely, if what they do leads to punishment, it is less likely that they will be (8) m________________.

1. model
2. modeling
3. imitation
4. models
5. imitate
6. models
7. imitated
8. modeled

EXAMPLE OF MODELING AND IMITATION WITH CHILDREN

Authors: Bandura, A., Ross, D., & Ross, S.A.

Title: Imitation of film-mediated aggressive models.

Source: *Journal of Abnormal and Social Psychology,* 1963, 66, 3-11.

Behavior: Aggression.

Modeling: Observation of aggression.

The boy's been watching too much television again, Mary!

Imitation is one of the strongest modes of learning complicated behavior we have, and children are born imitators. They often mimic behaviors they observe. There is concern about the modeling we present to our youth on TV and in movies, and the high content of violence. Do children learn aggression by just watching it? In this classic study, Bandura, Ross and Ross show that indeed they do.

One group of nursery school children watched a live adult model being aggressive with an inflatable BoBo doll. The model punched it, sat on it, and hit it with a mallet. A second group observed this aggression on a film, and a third group saw an animated cartoon of a cat character displaying the same kind of aggression. Afterwards, each child was taken to a playroom which had a BoBo doll and other toys, and was observed. All three modeling conditions taught the children aggression which they then displayed in their play. The children who were observers had learned to punch, sit on and hit the doll! Real life and film models did not differ substantially in their effect. Just observing an aggressive (1) m______________ (including films and cartoons) can teach aggression. (2) I______________ is a very strong mode of learning both desirable and undesirable social behavior.

1. model 2. imitation

EXAMPLE OF MODELING AND IMITATION WITH ADULTS

Authors: Wilson, F.S., & Walters, R.H.

Title: Modification of speech output of near-mute schizophrenics through social-learning procedures.

Source: *Behaviour Research and Therapy,* 1966, 4, 59-67.

Behavior: Frequency of talking.
Modeling: Observation of a talkative model.

Imitation is a potent mode of learning for adults as well as children. Wilson and Walters worked with 12 adult male schizophrenics in a hospital. They were rated as being particularly inactive and having a very low frequency of talking. The experimental condition was measuring number of words in describing color slides that were shown to them. They were divided into three groups: one simply observed a model who was very talkative in describing slides; a second group was both exposed to the model and reinforced with pennies for talking; and a control group was neither exposed to a model nor reinforced. Both the modeling only and the modeling plus reinforcement groups increased significantly in their speech frequency while the control group remained unchanged. Here a talkative (1) m____________ was used to increase the (2) f____________ of speech in near-mute schizophrenics.

---

1. model 2. frequency

PRACTICE PAGE

This is the way that I might use the Principle of Modeling and Imitation:

1. BEHAVIOR TO BE CHANGED:

2. HOW THIS BEHAVIOR COULD BE MEASURED:

3. BEHAVIORAL PLAN (How I might use *modeling* and *imitation* to change *this* behavior):

4. POSSIBLE ETHICAL AND LEGAL ISSUES:

Chapter 20

Principle of Self-Control

IN SELF-CONTROL PEOPLE CAN CHANGE THEIR OWN BEHAVIOR BY LEARNING TO MEASURE, EVALUATE AND REWARD OR PUNISH THEIR OWN BEHAVIOR.

People can make changes in their own environment. A woman who is concerned about her weight can paint a NO! on her refrigerator. In doing that she changes her (1) e________________. The next time she goes to the refrigerator to get some food, the NO! she put there may stop her from opening the door. We call this process (2) s________________-c________________. She has controlled her environment which in turn has changed her behavior.

Stimuli or clues which lead to desired behavior can be arranged so that the behavior will have a great likelihood of occurring. You can leave only today's work on your desk, with nothing else to distract you. Or, you can purposely avoid (3) s________________ and clues which usually lead to an undesired behavior. Someone doesn't want to smoke so she (4) d________________ keep any cigarettes in the house.

Self-measurement can play a key role in self-control as well. Carrying a card or wearing a wrist counter and keeping a count of the number of assertive statements you make may alone serve as a reminder, and (5) i________________ your assertiveness.

Finally, people can reward and punish their own (6) b________________ A student can plan to take ten-minute breaks only after he reads 20 pages of his book. A child can learn to say "I'm doing well!" to herself, even without a parent around. In this last example, called "cognitive self-control," thoughts or (7) c________________ processes can also be brought under self-control.

---

1. environment
2. self-control
3. stimuli
4. doesn't
5. increase
6. behavior
7. cognitive

EXAMPLE OF SELF-CONTROL WITH CHILDREN

Authors: Meichenbaum, D.H., & Goodman, J.
Title: Training impulsive children to talk to themselves: A means of developing self-control.
Source: *Journal of Abnormal Psychology,* 1971, 77, 115-126.
Behavior: Test performance and classroom behavior.
Self-Control: Talking to self, self-instruction, self-reinforcement.

In this classic study Meichenbaum and Goodman trained a group of second graders who were exhibiting hyperactivity and poor self-control, to improve their behavior by talking to themselves. First, they watched and heard an adult take several tests while talking out loud about how he was proceeding, finishing, and finally, rewarding himself: "Even if I make an error, I can go slowly and carefully . . . Good." Next, each child took tests while saying such things out loud to himself, and finally took tests while talking only to himself (covertly). This group of children improved significantly more than control groups. In this study impulsive children learned to (1) c____________ themselves by (2) t____________ to themselves, first out loud and finally, (3) c____________.

1. control 2. talking 3. covertly

EXAMPLE OF SELF-CONTROL WITH ADULTS

Author: Mahoney, M.J.
Title: Self-reward and self-monitoring techniques for weight control.
Source: *Behavior Therapy,* 1974, 5, 48-57.

Behavior: Eating in obese adults.
Self-Control: Self-monitoring and self-reward.

Self-control can play a key role in weight control programs. In this study Mahoney compared the weight losses of obese adults who had different self-control programs. One group simply self-monitored their weight and eating habits. They had only brief and variable weight losses. Another group, who used this self-monitoring and also rewarded themselves for progress, showed greater weight loss improvements. Results suggest that while self-measuring alone can have some effect, (1) s______________-m______________ and (2) s______________-r______________ are more effective.

1. self-measuring 2. self-reward

PRACTICE PAGE

This is the way that I might use the Principle of Self-Control:

1. BEHAVIOR TO BE CHANGED:

2. HOW THIS BEHAVIOR COULD BE MEASURED:

3. BEHAVIORAL PLAN (How I might use *self-control* to change *this* behavior):

4. POSSIBLE ETHICAL AND LEGAL ISSUES:

Chapter 21

Principle of Token Economies

IN *COMPREHENSIVE* REINFORCEMENT SYSTEMS CALLED *TOKEN ECONOMIES,* TOKENS ARE EARNED AND LOST CONTINGENTLY FOR A VARIETY OF BEHAVIORS, AND THE TOKENS MAY BE EXCHANGED LATER FOR A VARIETY OF "BACK-UP" REINFORCERS.

A *comprehensive, total* reinforcement system called a (1) t____________ e____________ can be set up for an entire school classroom, a whole psychiatric hospital ward, a whole prison, or for an entire residential treatment center. (2) T____________ are simply tangible objects that can be earned in a variety of predetermined ways depending on the particular token economy. Tokens commonly used are poker chips, points, coins, play money, punches on cards, stars, etc. In a hospital, for example, five tokens may be earned by attending ward meetings each day. In this case the five tokens would be (3) p____________ r____________ intended to increase the rate of attending ward meetings.

Much like money, tokens can usually be saved, spent or lost. In token economies the tokens can usually be spent on a variety of "back-up" reinforcers like free time, special privileges, snacks, etc. – much like money can buy a number of things we want. These (4) "b________-u________" reinforcers actually *back up* the value of the tokens. Tokens can also be taken away or be fined at a predetermined rate for unwanted or destructive behavior. If fighting resulted in a fine or cost of 10 points in a token economy classroom, this would be an example of a particular kind of punishment: (5) r____________ c________ (see Chapter 14).

Token economies are *motivational* systems, much like miniature societies in which people "earn their own way" by (6) e____________ and (7) l____________ tokens contingent on their behavior. However, token economies are highly controlled environments, more highly controlled than usual life in the community. Therefore, generalization (see Chapter 9) can be a problem in that behaviors learned in this highly structured environment may not (8) g____________ to living outside, once the patient or prisoner is discharged or once a student returns to a "regular" classroom.

One answer to the problem is the gradual *fading out* of the token economy, for example, in a half-way house or an only somewhat controlled environment, in order to insure generalization to the new (9) e______________. There, for example, tokens could be earned for going to a regular school, for going to see the counselor, or for going to a regular job. Later, the regular contingencies *naturally* operating in the community, like working for pay, seeking and receiving help, and earning good grades and learning new things may be (10) t________ e_____________ enough to maintain adaptive behavior.

---

1. token economy
2. tokens
3. positive reinforcement
4. "back-up"
5. response cost
6. earning
7. losing
8. generalize
9. environment
10. token economy

EXAMPLE OF TOKEN ECONOMY WITH CHILDREN

Authors: Phillips, E.L., Phillips, E.A., Fixsen, D.L., & Wolf, M.M.
Title: Achievement Place: Behavior shaping works for delinquents.
Source: *Psychology Today,* June 1973, pp. 74-79.
Behavior: Wide range of behavior of predelinquents.
Token Economy: Earning and losing points in home-like setting.

In a residential treatment home for predelinquents, the authors show that the token economy principle can be successfully applied in a "home-style" setting within the community. Eight to twelve boys who have been placed at Achievement Place by the court, live with a set of professional "teaching parents." Tokens or points are earned or lost for a variety of behaviors, from academic progress in the regular school they attend to chores at home and social behavior between the boys. Points are "backed-up" with a wide choice of privileges, from use of telephone to snacks and allowance. The point system is gradually faded out to a merit system in preparation for returning to their own homes. In this successful (1) t__________ e__________, predelinquents earn and lose tokens or points for a variety of academic and social (2) b__________. The token or point system is gradually faded out to prepare the boys for leaving in order to help insure (3) g__________.

1. token economy 2. behaviors 3. generalization

EXAMPLE OF TOKEN ECONOMY WITH ADULTS

Authors: Ayllon, T., & Azrin, N.H.
Title: The measurement and reinforcement of behavior of psychotics.
Source: *Journal of the Experimental Analysis of Behavior,* 1965, 8, 357-383.
Behavior: Work performance by patients.
Token Economy: Earn tokens, spend them for a variety of reinforcers.

In this grandfather of all token economies, Ayllon and Azrin began to show the potency of tokens in what had been a "back ward" in a state hospital. Tokens were established as generalized reinforcers that could be exchanged for a variety of "back-up" reinforcers in six general categories: privacy, leave from the ward, social interaction with staff, religious activities, recreation, and commissary items. For example: the most desirable room cost 30 tokens, one choice of TV program cost three tokens, cigarettes or candy cost from one to five tokens. The behavior under study was work performance and work preference. The series of well-controlled studies showed that both amount of work and preference for jobs were dramatically controlled by token reinforcement. In this early study, tokens or (1) g____________ reinforcers were used with a variety of potent (2) "b__________-u________" reinforcers. Both amount of work and choice of jobs were controlled by (3) t____________ reinforcement.

1. generalized 2. "back-up" 3. token

PRACTICE PAGE

This is the way I might use the Principle of Token Economies:

1. BEHAVIOR TO BE CHANGED:

2. HOW THIS BEHAVIOR COULD BE MEASURED:

3. BEHAVIORAL PLAN (How I might use a *token economy* in changing *this* behavior):

4. POSSIBLE ETHICAL AND LEGAL ISSUES:

Chapter 22

Principle of Aversive Conditioning

IF *NEUTRAL* OR *POSITIVE* STIMULI ARE REPEATEDLY PAIRED WITH STRONGLY *AVERSIVE* STIMULI, THE ORIGINAL STIMULI WILL LOSE THEIR NEUTRAL OR POSITIVE STATUS AND WILL BE AVOIDED.

Many bad habits or unwanted behaviors, like smoking, alcoholism and sexual deviations have been eliminated with (1) a________________ conditioning. In aversive (2) c________________ the stimuli which lead to the bad habits are repeatedly paired or made to occur with noxious or (3) a________________ stimuli. The usual response to aversive (4) s________________ is to avoid or escape them, to stay away from them. For example, we usually (5) a________________ electric shock. Electric shock is (6) a________________ to us.

If we are trying to break a cigarette smoking habit, we might use (7) a________________ c________________. If we received an electric (8) s________________ each time we saw, touched and lighted a cigarette, we would gradually build up an aversion to cigarette (9) s________________. In this case seeing, touching and lighting a cigarette are (10) s________________ which used to lead to smoking (11) b________________. After several sessions of aversive conditioning, these same stimuli will lead to (12) a________________ cigarettes.

In addition to (13) a________________ c________________ taking place, with the repeated pairings of shock and smoking stimuli (seeing, touching, lighting cigarettes), punishment (Chapter 12) is at work as well, since smoking behavior leads to painful consequences. This (14) p________________ will add to the avoidance of smoking. (There are many important ethical considerations involved in using any painful stimuli; you should review the issues regarding this principle in the Introduction.)

---

1. aversive
2. conditioning
3. aversive
4. stimuli
5. avoid
6. aversive
7. aversive conditioning
8. shock
9. smoking
10. stimuli
11. behavior
12. avoiding
13. aversive conditioning
14. punishment

EXAMPLE OF AVERSIVE CONDITIONING WITH CHILDREN

Authors: MacCulloch, M.J., Williams, C., & Birtles, C.J.

Title: The successful application of aversion therapy to an adolescent exhibitionist.

Source: *Journal of Behavior Therapy and Experimental Psychiatry,* 1971, 2, 61-66.

Behavior: Exhibitionism.

Conditioning: Repeated pairing of electric shock with pictures of adult females.

This is a study of the treatment of a 12-year-old who was getting into trouble because he often exposed himself to older women. He was facing a court appearance, and a rapid means of stopping the behavior was needed. A slide projector and shock apparatus were set up so that a shock would follow viewing an older female. Done repeatedly, this would develop a sexual *aversion* toward older women.

The shock could be avoided by the boy pushing a button which removed the picture of the woman and replaced it with a girl closer to his age. Girls then became associated with pain avoidance and anxiety relief. Thus, he was being trained to sexually dislike or avoid older women, and learning not to be afraid of girls. In 18 such sessions he stopped exhibiting himself, was able to prevent exhibitory fantasies and became more interested in girls. At the five-month follow-up he was avoiding trouble and had a 13-year-old girl friend. Here, an (1) a_______________ to older females was developed by repeatedly pairing pictures of women with electric (2) s_______________ over several sessions.

1. aversion 2. shock

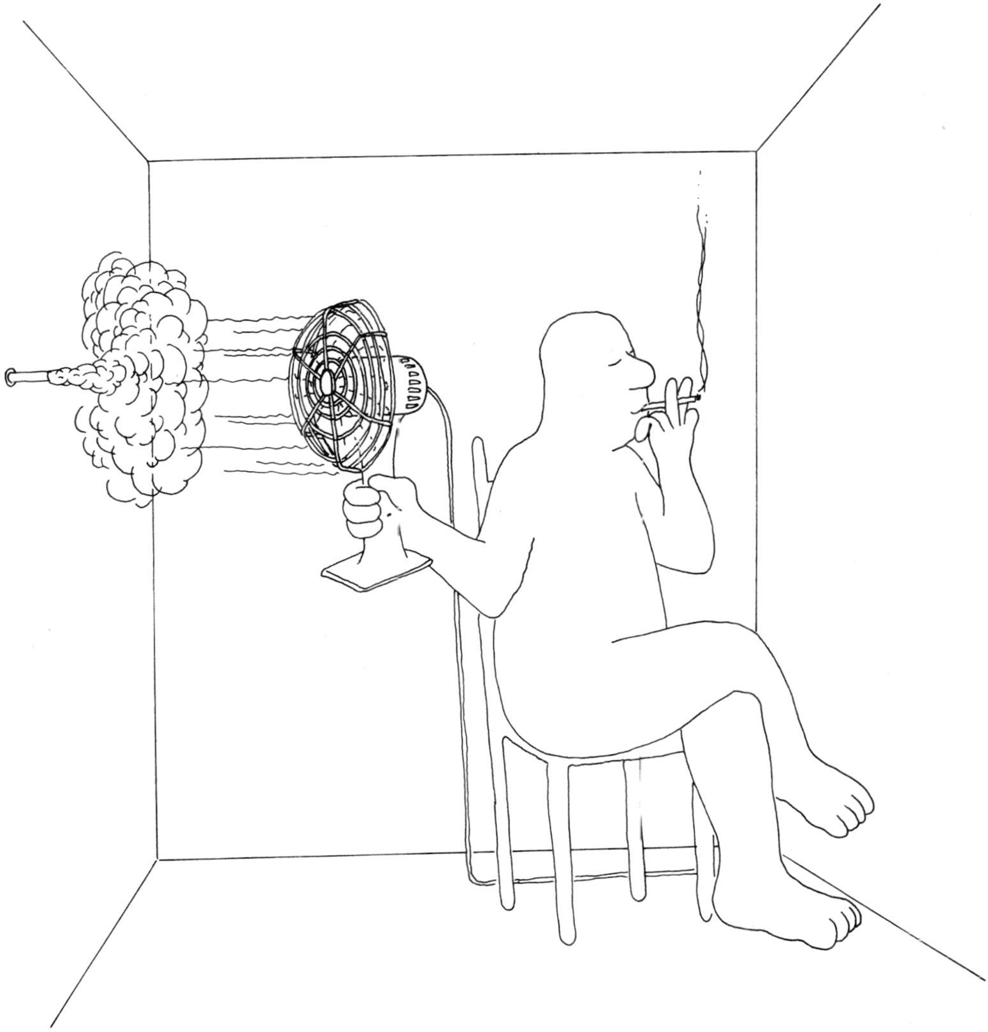

EXAMPLE OF AVERSIVE CONDITIONING WITH ADULTS

Authors: Franks, C., Fried, R., & Ashem, B.

Title: An improved apparatus for the aversive conditioning of smokers.

Source: *Behaviour Research and Therapy,* 1966, 4, 301-308.

Behavior: Smoking.

Conditioning: Pairing of smoking and hot smoke blown into the face.

These investigators developed an apparatus which would repeatedly blow hot smoke into the face of a person who was smoking, and blow fresh air when the cigarette was put out. Nine adult volunteers completed 12 sessions of this kind. They all experienced the hot-smoke sessions as very aversive. Of the eight reporting follow-up progress, four were not smoking anymore, one was smoking less, one had switched to a pipe, and two continued at their usual level. With repeated pairing of smoking behavior and aversive hot smoke blown into the face, we would expect an (1) a______________ to smoking to develop. Both aversive conditioning and (2) p______________ were at work. In addition, the fresh air blown into the face when a cigarette was put out was probably a positive (3) r______________.

---

1. aversion 2. punishment 3. reinforcer

PRACTICE PAGE

This is the way that I might use the Principle of Aversive Conditioning:

1. BEHAVIOR TO BE CHANGED:

2. HOW THIS BEHAVIOR COULD BE MEASURED:

3. BEHAVIORAL PLAN (How I might use *aversive conditioning* to change *this* behavior):

4. POSSIBLE ETHICAL AND LEGAL ISSUES:

REFERENCES

CHAPTER 1 / INTRODUCTION

Ayllon, T., & Azrin, N.H. The measurement and reinforcement of behavior of psychotics. *Journal of the Experimental Analysis of Behavior,* 1965, 8, 357-383.

Ayllon, T., & Azrin, N.H. *The token economy.* New York: Appleton-Century-Crofts, 1968.

Ayllon, T., & Michael, J. The psychiatric nurse as a behavioral engineer. *Journal of the Experimental Analysis of Behavior,* 1959, 3, 324-334.

Bachrach, A.J. Some applications of operant conditioning to behavior therapy. In J. Wolpe, A. Salter, & L.J. Reyna (Eds.), *The conditioning therapies.* New York: Holt, 1965, pp. 62-78.

Baer, D.M., & Wolf, M. The reinforcement contingency in preschool and remedial education. In R.D. Hess & R.M. Bear (Eds.), *Early education: Current theory, research, and action.* Chicago: Aldine, 1968, pp. 119-129.

Baer, D.M., Wolf, M.M., & Risley, T.R. Some current dimensions of applied behavior analysis. *Journal of Applied Behavior Analysis,* 1968, 1, 91-97.

Bandura, A. Social learning through imitation. In M.R. Jones (Ed.), *Nebraska Symposium on Motivation.* Lincoln: University of Nebraska Press, 1962, pp. 211-269.

Bandura, A. *Principles of behavior modification.* New York: Holt, 1969.

Bandura, A. (Ed.). *Psychological modeling: Conflicting theories.* Chicago: Aldine, 1975.

Becker, W.C. *Parents are teachers.* Champaign, IL: Research Press, 1971.

Birk, L., Stoltz, S.B., Brady, J.P., Brady, J.V., Lazarus, A.A., Lynch, J.J., Rosenthal, A.J., Skelton, W.D., Stevens, J.B., & Thomas, E.J. *Behavior therapy in psychiatry.* Washington, D.C.: American Psychiatric Association, 1973.

Bishop, B.R. Self-control is learned: External control precedes internal control. In J.S. Stumphauzer (Ed.), *Behavior therapy with delinquents.* Springfield, IL: Charles C. Thomas, 1973, pp. 54-65.

Brady, J.P. The ethics of behavior therapy. *Medical World News* (Psychiatry), October 1974, pp. 26-27.

Braun, S.H. Ethical issues in behavior modification. *Behavior Therapy,* 1975, 6, 51-62.

Buehler, R.E. Social reinforcement experimentation in open social systems. In J.S. Stumphauzer (Ed.), *Behavior therapy with delinquents.* Springfield, IL: Charles C. Thomas, 1973, pp. 250-262.

Burkhart, B.R., Behles, M.W., & Stumphauzer, J.S. Training juvenile probation officers in behavior modification: Knowledge, attitude change, or behavioral competence? *Behavior Therapy,* 1976, 7, 47-53.

Cautela, J.R. Statement in favor of certification. *Association for Advancement of Behavior Therapy Newsletter,* 1975, 2, 3-5.

Clark, R.N., Burgess, R.L., & Hendee, J.C. The development of anti-litter behavior in a forest campground. *Journal of Applied Behavior Analysis,* 1972, 5, 1-5.

Dollard, J., & Miller, N.E. *Personality and psychotherapy.* New York: McGraw-Hill, 1950.

Ellis, A. *Reason and emotion in psychotherapy.* New York: Lyle Stuart, 1962.

Ernst, F.A. Behavior therapy and training in clinical psychology: A student's perspective. *Journal of Behavior Therapy and Experimental Psychiatry,* 1971, 2, 15-74.

Evans, J.L. *Principles of programmed learning.* Riverside, CA: Teaching Machines, Inc., 1961.

Eysenck, H.J. The effects of psychotherapy: An evaluation. *Journal of Consulting Psychology,* 1952, 16, 319-324.

Eysenck, H.J. Learning theory and behavior therapy. *Journal of Mental Science,* 1959, 105, 61-75.

Ferster, C. D., & DeMyer, M.K. The development of performances in autistic children in an automatically controlled environment. *Journal of Chronic Disease,* 1961, 13, 312-345.

Franks, C.M. (Ed.). *Conditioning techniques in clinical practice.* New York: Springer, 1964.

Franks, C.M. (Ed.). *Behavior therapy: Appraisal and status.* New York: McGraw-Hill, 1969.

Franks, C.M., & Wilson, G.T. (Eds.). *Annual review of behavior therapy.* New York: Brunner/Mazel, 1973-1976.

Goldfried, M.R., Decenteceo, E.T., & Weinberg, L. Systematic rational restructuring as a self-control technique. *Behavior Therapy,* 1974, 5, 247-254.

Jones, M.C. A laboratory study of fear: The case of Peter. *Journal of Genetic Psychology,* 1924, 31, 308-315.

Kanfer, F.H., & Phillips, J.S. *Learning foundations of behavior therapy.* New York: Wiley, 1970.

Kazdin, A.E., & Bootzin, R.R. The token economy: An evaluative review. *Journal of Applied Behavior Analysis,* 1972, 5, 343-372.

Krasner, L. Behavior therapy. *Annual Review of Psychology,* 1971, 22, 483-532.

Krasner, L., & Ullmann, L.P. (Eds.). *Research in behavior modification.* New York: Holt, 1965.

Lazarus, A.A. New methods in psychotherapy: A case study. *South African Medical Journal,* 1958, 33, 660.

Lazarus, A.A. A plea for technical and theoretical breadth. *Association for Advancement of Behavior Therapy Newsletter,* 1968, 3, 2.

Lazarus, A.A. *Behavior therapy and beyond.* New York: McGraw-Hill, 1971.

Lee, A.L., & Jacobs, G. Workshop airs patients' rights. *Hospitals,* 1973, 47, 39-43.

Lindsley, O.R., & Skinner, B.F. A method for the experimental analysis of the behavior of psychotic patients. *American Psychologist,* 1954, 9, 419-420.

Lovaas, O.I., Schaeffer, B., & Simmons, J.Q. Building social behavior in autistic children by use of electric shock. *Journal of Experimental Research in Personality,* 1965, 1, 99-109.

Lucero, J.R., Vail, D.H., & Scherber, J. Regulating operant conditioning programs. *Hospital & Community Psychiatry,* 1968, 19, 53-54.

Malott, R.W., & Hartlep, P. *Contingency management in education.* Kalamazoo, MI: Behaviordelia, 1972.

Marmor, J. Dynamic psychotherapy and behavior therapy: Are they irreconcilable? *Archives of General Psychiatry,* 1971, 24, 22-28.

Martin, R. *Legal challenges to behavior modification in schools, corrections, and mental health.* Champaign, IL: Research Press, 1975.

Masserman, J.H. *Behavior and neurosis.* Chicago: University of Chicago Press, 1943.

Meichenbaum, D.H. Toward a cognitive theory of self-control (Research Report No. 48). Waterloo, Ontario: University of Waterloo, Psychology Department, 1975.

Meichenbaum, D.H., & Goodman, J. Training impulsive children to talk to themselves. *Journal of Abnormal Psychology,* 1971, 77, 115-126.

Meichenbaum, D.H., & Cameron, R. Training schizophrenics to talk to themselves: A means of developing attentional controls. *Behavior Therapy,* 1973, 4, 515-534.

Miller, N.E. Learning of visceral and glandular responses. *Science,* 1969, 163, 434-445.

Miller, N.E. Interactions between learned and physical factors in mental illness. *Seminars In Psychiatry,* 1972, 4, No. 3.

Mowrer, O.H., & Mowrer, W.A. Enuresis: A method for its study and treatment. *American Journal of Orthopsychiatry,* 1938, 8, 436-447.

Neisworth, J.T., & Smith, R.M. *Modifying retarded behavior.* Boston: Houghton Mifflin, 1973.

O'Leary, K.D., & O'Leary, S.G. (Eds.). *Classroom management: The successful use of behavior modification.* New York: Pergamon, 1972.

Patterson, G.R. Recent trends in behavior modification with children. Paper given at Western Psychological Association Convention, San Francisco, April 23, 1971. (a)

Patterson, G.R. *Families: Applications of social learning to family life.* Champaign, IL: Research Press, 1971. (b)

Paul, G.L. Behavior modification research: design and tactics. In C.M. Franks (Ed.), *Behavior therapy: Appraisal and status.* New York: McGraw-Hill, 1969, pp. 29-62.

Pavlov, I.P. *Conditioned reflexes: An investigation of the physiological activity of the cerebral cortex.* London: Oxford, 1927.

Pavlov, I.P. *Lectures on conditioned reflexes* (Vol. 1). London: Lawrence and Wishart, 1928.

Pavlov, I.P. Neuroses in man and animals. *Journal of the American Medical Association,* 1932, 99, 1012-1013.

Pavlov, I.P. *Conditioned reflexes and psychiatry.* New York: International, 1941.

Rimm, D.C., & Masters, J.C. *Behavior therapy: Techniques and empirical findings.* New York: Academic Press, 1974.

Salter, A. *Conditioned reflex therapy.* New York: Farrar, Straus, 1949.

Schaefer, H.H., & Martin, P.L. *Behavioral therapy.* New York: McGraw-Hill, 1969.

Schwitzgebel, R.K. *Development and legal regulation of coercive behavior modification techniques with offenders.* Chevy Chase, MD: National Institute of Mental Health, 1971.

Schwitzgebel, R.L., & Schwitzgebel, R.K. (Eds.). *Psychotechnology: Electronic control of mind and behavior.* New York: Holt, 1973.

Shectman, F.A. Operant conditioning and psychoanalysis: Contrasts, similarities, and some thoughts about integration. *American Journal of Psychotherapy,* 1975, 29, 72-78.

Skinner, B.F. *The behavior of organisms.* New York: Appleton-Century-Crofts, 1938.

Skinner, B.F. *Walden two.* New York: Macmillan, 1948.

Skinner, B.F. *Science and human behavior.* New York: Macmillan, 1953.

Skinner, B.F. *Beyond freedom and dignity.* New York: Knopf, 1971.

Skinner, B.F. *About behaviorism.* New York: Knopf, 1974.

Skinner, B.F., & Lindsley, O.R. Studies in behavior therapy (Status reports II and III, Contract N5 ori-7662). Washington, D.C.: Office of Naval Research, 1954.

Smith, A.B. Humanism and behavior modification: Is there a conflict? *The Elementary School Journal,* 1973, 74, 59-67.

Stein, T.J. Some ethical considerations of short-term workshops in the principles and methods of behavior modification. *Journal of Applied Behavior Analysis,* 1975, 8, 113-115.

Stuart, R.B. Statement opposed to certification. *Association for Advancement of Behavior Therapy Newsletter,* 1975, 2, No. 1, 1-3. (a)

Stuart, R.B. President's message. *Association for Advancement of Behavior Therapy Newsletter,* 1975, 2, No. 2, 1-2. (b)

Stumphauzer, J.S. *Daily behavior graph manual.* Venice, CA: Behaviormetrics, 1972.

Stumphauzer, J.S. (Ed.). *Behavior therapy with delinquents.* Springfield, IL: Charles C. Thomas, 1973.

Stumphauzer, J.S. *Daily behavior card manual.* Venice, CA: Behaviormetrics, 1974. (a)

Stumphauzer, J.S. *Six techniques of modifying delinquent behavior.* Leonia, NJ: Behavioral Sciences Tape Library, 1974. (b)

Stumphauzer, J.S. Modifying delinquent behavior: Beginnings and current practices. *Adolescence,* 1976, 11, 13-28.

Stumphauzer, J.S. (Ed.). *Progress in behavior therapy with delinquents.* Springfield, IL: Charles C. Thomas, in press.

Stumphauzer, J.S., Aiken, T.W., & Veloz, E.V. "East side story": Behavioral analysis of a high juvenile crime community. In J.S. Stumphauzer (Ed.), *Progress in behavior therapy with delinquents.* Springfield, IL: Charles C. Thomas, in press.

Szasz, T.S. *The myth of mental illness.* New York: Hoeber, 1961.

Teicher, J.D., Sinay, R.D., & Stumphauzer, J.S. Training community-based paraprofessionals as behavior therapists with families of alcohol abusing adolescents. *American Journal of Psychiatry,* 1976, 133, 847-850.

Thorensen, C.E., & Mahoney, M.J. *Behavioral self-control.* New York: Holt, 1974.

Thorndike, E.L. *The psychology of learning.* New York: Teachers College Press, 1913.

Ullmann, L.P., & Krasner, L. (Eds.). *Case studies in behavior modification.* New York: Holt, 1965.

Wahler, R.G., Winkel, G.H., Peterson, R.F., & Morrison, D.C. Mothers as behavior therapists for their own children. *Behaviour Research and Therapy,* 1965, 3, 113-124.

Watson, D.L., & Tharp, R.G. *Self-directed behavior: Self-modification for personal adjustment.* Belmont, CA: Brooks/Cole, 1972.

Watson, J.B. *Behaviorism.* New York: Norton, 1924.

Watson, J.B., & Rayner, R. Conditioned emotional reactions. *Journal of Experimental Psychology,* 1920, 3, 1-14.

Wolpe, J. Experimental neurosis as learned behavior. *British Journal of Psychology,* 1952, 43, 243.

Wolpe, J. *Psychotherapy by reciprocal inhibition.* Stanford: Stanford University Press, 1958.

Wolpe, J. *The practice of behavior therapy.* New York: Pergamon, 1969.

Wolpe, J. *The practice of behavior therapy* (2nd ed.). New York: Pergamon, 1973.

Wolpe, J. Behavior therapy and its malcontents – I. Denial of its bases and psychodynamic fusionism. *Journal of Behavior Therapy and Experimental Psychiatry,* 1976, 7, 1-5. (a)

Wolpe, J. Behavior therapy and its malcontents – II. Multimodal eclecticism, cognitive exclusivism, and "exposure" empiricism. *Journal of Behavior Therapy and Experimental Psychiatry,* 1976, 7, 109-116. (b)

Wolpe, J. *Theme and variation: A behavior therapy casebook.* New York: Pergamon, 1976. (c)

Wolpe, J., & Lazarus, A.A. *Behavior therapy techniques.* New York: Pergamon 1966.

Yates, A.J. *Behavior therapy.* New York: Wiley, 1970.

CHAPTER 2 / PRINCIPLE OF BEHAVIORAL ANALYSIS

Buehler, R.E., Patterson, G.R., & Furniss, J.M. The reinforcement of behavior in institutional settings. *Behaviour Research and Therapy,* 1966, 4, 157-167.

Cautela, J.R., & Kastenbaum, R. A reinforcement survey schedule for use in therapy, training, and research. *Psychological Reports,* 1967, 20, 1115-1130.

CHAPTER 3 / PRINCIPLE OF BEHAVIOR MEASUREMENT

Bailey, J.S., Wolf, M.M., & Phillips, E.L. Home-based reinforcement and the modification of predelinquents' classroom behavior. *Journal of Applied Behavior Analysis,* 1970, 3, 223-233.

Maletzky, B.M. Behavior recording as treatment: A brief note. *Behavior Therapy,* 1974, 5, 107-111.

CHAPTER 4 / PRINCIPLE OF POSITIVE REINFORCEMENT

Azrin, N.H., & Lindsley, O.R. The reinforcement of cooperation between children. *Journal of Abnormal and Social Psychology,* 1956, 52, 100-102.

Stumphauzer, J.S. Application of reinforcement contingencies with a 23-year-old anorexic patient. *Psychological Reports,* 1969, 24, 109-110.

CHAPTER 5 / PRINCIPLE OF NEGATIVE REINFORCEMENT

Azrin, N., Rubin, H., O'Brian, F., Ayllon, T., & Roll, D. Behavioral engineering: Postural control by a portable operant apparatus. *Journal of Applied Behavior Analysis,* 1968, 1, 99-108.

Lovaas, O.I., Schaeffer, B., & Simmons, J.Q. Building social behavior in autistic children by use of electric shock. *Journal of Experimental Research in Personality,* 1965, 1, 99-109.

CHAPTER 6 / PRINCIPLE OF SHAPING

Ayllon, T., & Haughton, E. Control of the behavior of schizophrenic patients by food. *Journal of the Experimental Analysis of Behavior,* 1962, 5, 343-352.

Lovaas, O.I., Berberich, J., Perloff, B., & Schaeffer, B. Acquisition of imitative speech by schizophrenic children. *Science,* 1966, 162, 705-707.

CHAPTER 7 / PRINCIPLE OF SCHEDULES OF REINFORCEMENT

Hopkins, B.L. Effects of candy and social reinforcement, instructions and reinforcement schedule leaning on the modification and maintenance of smiling. *Journal of Applied Behavior Analysis,* 1968, 1, 121-129.

Kazdin, A.E., & Polster, R. Intermittent token reinforcement and response maintenance in extinction. *Behavior Therapy,* 1973, 4, 386-391.

CHAPTER 8 / PRINCIPLE OF SOCIAL REINFORCEMENT

Stumphauzer, J.S. Modification of delay choices in institutionalized youthful offenders through social reinforcement. *Psychonomic Science,* 1970, 18, 222-223.

Thomas, D.A., Nielson, L.J., Kuypers, D.S., & Becker, W.C. Social reinforcement and remedial instruction in the elimination of a classroom behavior problem. *The Journal of Special Education,* 1968, 2, 291-305.

CHAPTER 9 / PRINCIPLE OF GENERALIZATION

Blanchard, E.D., & Johnson, R.A. Generalization of operant classroom control procedures. *Behavior Therapy,* 1973, 4, 219-229.

Kale, R.I., Kaye, J., Whelan, P., & Hopkins, B.L. The effects of reinforcement on the modification, maintenance and generalization of social responses of mental patients. *Journal of Applied Behavior Analysis,* 1968, 1, 307-314.

CHAPTER 10 / PREMACK PRINCIPLE

Gupton, T., & LeBow, M.D. Behavior management in a large industrial firm. *Behavior Therapy,* 1971, 2, 78-82.

Homme, L., deBaca, P., Devine, J., Steinhorst, R., & Rickert, E. Use of the Premack Principle in controlling the behavior of nursery school children. *Journal of the Experimental Analysis of Behavior,* 1963, 6, 544.

CHAPTER 11 / PRINCIPLE OF ASSERTION TRAINING

Bloomfield, H.H. Assertive training in an outpatient group of chronic schizophrenics: A preliminary report. *Behavior Therapy,* 1973, 4, 277-281.

Gittelman, M. Behavior rehearsal as a technique in child treatment. *Journal of Child Psychology and Psychiatry,* 1965, 6, 251-255.

CHAPTER 12 / PRINCIPLE OF PUNISHMENT 1: AVERSIVE STIMULATION

Kohlenberg, R.J. The punishment of persistent vomiting: A case study. *Journal of Applied Behavior Analysis,* 1970, 3, 241-245.

O'Leary, K.D., Kaufman, K.F., Kass, R.E., & Drabman, R.S. The effects of loud and soft reprimands on the behavior of disruptive students. *Exceptional Children,* 1970, 37, 145-155.

CHAPTER 13 / PRINCIPLE OF PUNISHMENT 2: TIME-OUT

Adams, M.R., & Popelka, G. The influence of "time-out" on stutterers and their dysfluency. *Behavior Therapy,* 1971, 2, 234-239.

Bishop, B.R., & Stumphauzer, J.S. Behavior therapy of thumbsucking in children: A punishment (time-out) and generalization effect – what's a mother to do? *Psychological Reports,* 1973, 33, 939-944.

CHAPTER 14 / PRINCIPLE OF PUNISHMENT 3: RESPONSE COST

Harmatz, M.G., & Lapuc, P. Behavior modification of overeating in a psychiatric population. *Journal of Consulting and Clinical Psychology,* 1968, 32, 583-587.

Kaufman, K.F., & O'Leary, K.D. Reward, cost, and self-evaluation procedures for disruptive adolescents in a psychiatric hospital school. *Journal of Applied Behavior Analysis,* 1972, 5, 293-309.

CHAPTER 15 / PRINCIPLE OF EXTINCTION

Agras, W.S. Behavior therapy in the management of chronic schizophrenia. *American Journal of Psychiatry,* 1967, 124, 240-243.

Zimmerman, E.H., & Zimmerman, J. The alteration of behavior in a special classroom situation. *Journal of the Experimental Analysis of Behavior,* 1962, 5, 59-60.

CHAPTER 16 / PRINCIPLE OF COUNTERCONDITIONING

Lazarus, A.A., & Abramovitz, A. The use of "emotive imagery" in the treatment of children's phobias. *Journal of Mental Science,* 1962, 108, 191-195.

Wolpe, J. The systematic desensitization treatment of neuroses. *The Journal of Nervous and Mental Disease,* 1961, 132, 189-203.

CHAPTER 17 / PRINCIPLE OF NEGATIVE PRACTICE

Keutzer, C.S. Behavior modification of smoking: The experimental investigation of diverse techniques. *Behaviour Research and Therapy,* 1968, 6, 137-157.

Walton, D. Experimental psychology and the treatment of a ticqueur. *Journal of Child Psychology and Psychiatry,* 1961, 2, 148-155.

CHAPTER 18 / PRINCIPLE OF DEPRIVATION AND SATIATION

Ayllon, T. Intensive treatment of psychotic behavior by stimulus satiation and food reinforcement. *Behaviour Research and Therapy,* 1963, 1, 53-61.

Lovaas, O.I., Freitag, G., Kindler, M.I., Rubenstein, B.D., Schaeffer, B., & Simmons, J.Q. Establishment of social reinforcers in schizophrenic children using food. *Journal of Experimental Child Psychology,* 1966, 4, 109-125.

CHAPTER 19 / PRINCIPLE OF MODELING AND IMITATION

Bandura, A., Ross, D., & Ross, S.A. Imitation of film-mediated aggressive models. *Journal of Abnormal and Social Psychology,* 1963, 66, 3-11.

Wilson, F.S., & Walters, R.H. Modification of speech output of near-mute schizophrenics through social-learning procedures. *Behaviour Research and Therapy,* 1966, 4, 59-67.

CHAPTER 20 / PRINCIPLE OF SELF-CONTROL

Mahoney, M.J. Self-reward and self-monitoring techniques for weight control. *Behavior Therapy,* 1974, 5, 48-57.

Meichenbaum, D.H., & Goodman, J. Training impulsive children to talk to themselves: A means of developing self-control. *Journal of Abnormal Psychology,* 1971, 77, 115-126.

CHAPTER 21 / PRINCIPLE OF TOKEN ECONOMIES

Ayllon, T., & Azrin, N.H. The measurement and reinforcement of behavior of psychotics. *Journal of the Experimental Analysis of Behavior,* 1965, 8, 357-383.

Phillips, E.L., Phillips, E.A., Fixsen, D.L., & Wolf, M.M. Achievement Place: Behavior shaping works for delinquents. *Psychology Today,* June 1973, pp. 74-79.

CHAPTER 22 / PRINCIPLE OF AVERSIVE CONDITIONING

Franks, C., Fried, R., & Ashem, B. An improved apparatus for the aversive conditioning of smokers. *Behaviour Research and Therapy,* 1966, 4, 301-308.

MacCulloch, M.J., Williams, C., & Birtles, C.J. The successful application of aversion therapy to an adolescent exhibitionist. *Journal of Behavior Therapy and Experimental Psychiatry,* 1971, 2, 61-66.

Name Index

Subject Index